MORNING RITUALS
for
A PRODUCTIVE AND SUCCESSFUL DAY

MORNING RITUALS
for
A PRODUCTIVE AND SUCCESSFUL DAY

Aruna Joshi

WAKE UP! Morning Rituals *for* A Productive and Successful Day
©Aruna Joshi 2017

First Edition 2017

Published in India by:
Embassy Book Distributors
120, Great Western Building,
Maharashtra Chamber of Commerce Lane,
Fort, Mumbai 400 023, India
Tel: (+9122) -30967415, 22819546
Email: info@embassybooks.in
www.embassybooks.in

ISBN: 978-81-933415-8-2

All rights reserved. No part of this publication may be reproduced, distributed, or transmitted in any form or by any means, including photocopying, recording, or other electronic or mechanical methods, without the prior written permission of the publisher. The use of brief quotations embodied in reviews is permitted.

Cover Design by Sonal Churi

Layout and typesetting by PSV Kumarasamy

DEDICATION

This book, to my dear parents, I dedicate
Which without their blessings, I could never create
They worked hard to give me the best
Despite life putting them on test after test
They inculcated in me moral values high
Which I cannot forget until I die
Their love and support gave my life a lift
To them I present this book as a gift

ACKNOWLEDGEMENT

I always dreamt of becoming a writer since I was a child. And now, I am actually living my dream! Thanks to the Almighty for showing me the way and making this happen!

As they say, there are no coincidences in life; everything happens for a reason. Every person we meet along the journey has a role to play in our life. A big 'Thank you' to each and everyone who has played that role in my life.

My husband Santosh has been my biggest strength and support, always encouraging me to follow my dreams. He says, "Discover your passion, follow your purpose and you will never regret". Today I can say, I have absolutely no regrets about anything in my life.

I am blessed to have my parents and my in-laws who are so supportive and encouraging.

My dear friend and publisher, Sohin Lakhani, who has turned my dream (this book), into a reality. I am indebted to him for igniting the spark of writing in me and showing confidence in my writing more than I did.

Sonal Churi for designing a fabulous cover.

There are some people who have been there through my life's journey and have touched my life in true sense and I would like to express my deepest gratitude to them—S.R. Marathe, Nitin Deshmukh, Suma Varughese, Vaishali Pedram, Baishali Bhattacharya, Priti Savoor, Madhu Sahoo, Shweta and Santa Thourani, Subir Patel, Meirah, Sakshi, Rinku, Jyotsna, Shivratan Singrodia, Sunil, Shabana, Kiran, my brother Aniruddha and his wife Arati, My sister-in-law Manisha, Kishor, and my entire family. Thank you all from the bottom of my heart.

Table of Content

PREFACE
Just a few minutes…   11

1   **WAKE UP AND FOLLOW YOUR DREAMS**
Well Begun Is Half Done   20

2   **ARE YOU A MORNING LARK, A NIGHT OWL OR A HUMMING BIRD?**
Quality Sleep Is Important   32

3   **WAKE UP TO FITNESS**
Humans Are Designed For Movement   40

4   **ENERGIZE WITH A SUPERFOOD BREAKFAST**
Don't Eat Less, Eat Right   64

5   **MEDITATE AND RELAX**
Quiet The Mind And The Soul Will Speak   78

6   **ISUALIZE THE DAY AHEAD**
Get, Set, Goals   88

7   **WAKE UP WITH A BOOSTER DOSE OF MOTIVATION**
Your Only Limit Is You   96

8	**MUSIC IS THE MEDICINE FOR MIND**	
	Integrate Music in your Life	106

9	**HAVE AN ATTITUDE OF GRATITUDE**	
	Thankful People Are Always Happy	112

10	**WAKING UP TO LIVE FULLY AND PASSIONATELY**	
	Make the Impossible Happen	120

11	**RISE AND SHINE**	
	Head-start Your Day	130

Preface

Just a few minutes...

"Just a few minutes......please, Mommy!" These words would buy me, that little extra time to extend my sleep.

This was how my morning started on most days while I was studying Architecture. I often worked late through the night, juggling with the project submission deadlines. Staying awake till early morning was a normal practice, but waking up to see the sunrise was a far-fetched reality for me.

Deep in the night, after I exhausted myself working, I would tell my mom who by then, would be in deep sleep after a day's hard work, "Mom, please wake me up at 5am. I need to complete my assignment." My mom would diligently set an alarm for quarter to five. She would wake up several times in the night, and check the clock, to make sure that she doesn't miss the alarm. She would lose her sleep over waking me up and I would sleep like a log. Finally, she would wake up at 4.30am, even before the alarm went off; come to my room and sleep besides me, to wake me up correctly at 5am. At ten minutes to five, gently stroking my head, she would say, "Wake up dear, its 5am" and my standard reply would

wake up

be, "Just a few minutes…..please, Mommy"; half asleep, I would hug her tightly and get lost in the dream world again.

After a few attempts of trying, my mom would leave me to sleep, and get busy with her morning chores. Then after a while, I would wake up startled with my pulse racing and feeling both anxious and guilty for having woken up late and lost the precious time.

My conversation for the day would start with, "Mom, why didn't you wake me up?" My mom would fret about the whole situation and get really mad at me, "why do you tell me to wake you up when you don't want to?" and add in a determined tone, "You are old enough now. Tomorrow onwards, you set your own alarm and wake up."

Just one hug and a promise to wake up at the first call from the next day was enough to her melt her buttery soft heart. And then my day would start with a steaming cup of ginger lemongrass tea, lovingly made by my mother. The aroma of the tea penetrating through all the cells would enliven and brighten me up to finish the balanced work. This routine continued for my entire college tenure. My mom never gave up on me and I never changed.

On the other hand, my brother who is younger to me by four years, would spring out of bed, even putting the roosters to shame. My mom never had to waste her precious morning energy to wake him up. It seemed as if I was the only odd one out in our family of six. My grand-parents who lived with us had a set routine. Their mornings would start rather too early. My grandma would be up, ready and out by 4.30am to attend the first Aarti at a nearby temple. She would come back totally charged up to start her day. My grandpa preferred to spend his early time of the morning reading and writing, after a short walk. For my dad, his day had to start with a one-hour long brisk walk followed by half an hour of Yoga, irrespective of whether it was harsh summer, severe winter or incessant rains. He loved to exercise no matter what.

Amidst all the morning larks in my family, I was the only night owl. All of them made futile efforts to change me to fit into their clan. My grandparents lectured me on the benefits of waking up early and how it has positive effects on our mind, body and soul. My dad would often express his unhappiness over the sedentary life-style I led and stressed on the importance of morning exercise. All these words carrying advice did enter through one ear but quickly left through the other, without even touching my brain.

My morning was rather set, until I was married. Wake up by 8am, have a cup of tea while reading a book or newspaper. This gave me the much needed quiet time before I started interacting with other people around. This also acted as a power stimulant for my body, mind and soul and set the tone for the day.

I have spent almost two and a half decades of my life living in a small to mid-sized town, where life is 'pretty chilled out'. People usually wake up early in the morning, practice some form of exercise, read newspapers, spend time with family and friends, before they set out to work. The distances are short and so is the time taken to reach to the destination. One doesn't have to really go through the ordeal of commuting; as is the case of the metros. That's the beauty of smaller cities; the day-to day challenges are minimal. The peaceful atmosphere, dense greenery, reduced pollution levels, less stress helps the people in these cities to live a healthy and serene life.

wake up

My war with the snooze button...

After my relocation to Mumbai post marriage, I went through a major cultural shock. The pace of life changed drastically and my regular morning routine went haywire. Living in Thane and commuting to Santacruz for work every morning, in the over-packed local trains was no less than a nightmare.

It used to take me two hours to commute one way. Moreover, being a married woman, I was encumbered with several responsibilities. I had to set up a completely new routine for myself. Before leaving home at seven in the morning, I cooked breakfast and lunch, packed lunch-boxes for my husband and myself, got ready and rushed down to catch an auto to the station.

In compliance to this new routine, I had to wake up at 5am. I was literally at war with the snooze button. Though I would try to hit the bed by 11pm, I would end up staring at the stars from my bed room window till past midnight. Being a night owl, it was impossible for me to sleep early.

Sometimes I would miss the train and reach late to office, or sometimes I would have to skip the breakfast and lunch if I woke up late. This left me feeling guilty as my husband would also have to go without it. Or, if everything went well, as per my new routine, then I would just doze off in the office, which was highly embarrassing. My energising morning cup of tea which was a power start to my morning routine for many years, had no place in my new routine. The first cup of tea I would have was, when I reached office.

My grandma's words would keep ringing in my ears, "you should get into the habit of waking up early. Its fine now, but life will be difficult for you after marriage." But my mom would quickly defend me saying, "Mamma, she studies till late in the night. You know how demanding the Architecture course is. I am sure she will manage well."

Each day was a huge challenge for me. I realised that I could not be turned into a 'morning person', but my routine demanded me to be one. I lost most of my energy trying to resolve this conflict. While people around me looked fresh and energetic in the mornings, I was groggy and complaining. This largely affected my nature, my productivity, my relationships and almost every aspect of my life. This continued for a few years.

The war ended...

Gradually, I switched to working independently, as I started my practise as an Architect & Interior designer. My morning routine changed once again. Now there were no pressures of leaving home early. I was my own boss, and could plan my day productively, around my peak energy hours. My day would start by waking up at 7am feeling fresh, savour my ginger-lemongrass tea, read a motivational book, take shower for good 15 minutes, meditate for a while, cook breakfast and lunch; and all this would be done by 9.30am and I would be ready to hit the gym.

Life started flowing smoothly again, and more importantly I was happy and energetic throughout the day. This happened because I changed my career settings and stopped trying hard to change myself. Instead I worked out a routine that best suited to my body clock. And this really worked in my favour.

wake up

If you don't drive your day your day will drive you...

We all have our own morning rituals that motivate us, that we religiously follow every day, that sets the tone for the entire day, that drives and pushes us to achieve our goals, that makes us happy and gives us confidence.

It is important to find out that 'driving force'. It could be a power walk, meditation, reading, writing, or even as simple as a steaming cup of tea or coffee. It is of utmost importance to find out that which gives a kick-start to your day. Something that has been there with you always, that which gives you power and confidence.

The phrase, 'Getting up from the wrong side of the bed', reiterates the importance of starting the day on a right note. Starting the day right, will not only make you feel in control of the day and the events that happen throughout the day, but will also keep you happy and positive. If you don't take charge and drive your day, then the day is sure to drive you.

As you sail through life, your morning routine may change, but the driving force remains the same. Off late, when I made a career shift to writing, I realized that morning time is my best time to write, especially as soon as I wake up. Best of my writings have happened then. Words just flow through me effortlessly during that time. But this did not change me in to a morning person. Power time for me, is whatever time I wake in the morning after a good night's sleep. I am just harnessing my power time to achieve my goals. Now I have made further amendments to my morning routine.

I do some stretching while still on bed. This limbers the muscles and joints and enhances the blood flow throughout the body providing an extra shot of oxygen to all the tissues of the body. I drink almost 3 glasses of water, make my special tea and sit with my laptop and pour out my thoughts. If I am not in a mood to write than I utilize that time to read. Everything else comes after that.

I have realized, that several new morning routines have come into my life at every juncture, but my morning cup of tea and that quiet time with myself is irreplaceable.

The most important thing in life is adaptability. It is difficult to fix up a morning routine and follow it throughout your life. Everything in life requires an update and so does the morning routine. It changes when you step out from school to college to job to marriage to starting a family. It needs a complete make over with the change in place, culture, age, people you are living with, climate, job profile, economic conditions, social and family responsibilities and so on.

What to expect from this book?

This book talks about the importance of the start of the day. It explores various morning routines that successful people follow. It answers the 'whys' and 'hows' of each ritual to be followed in the morning. It helps you discover yourself, and know yourself better; so that you can plan a perfect morning routine for yourself. Following a morning routine will make your day most productive and successful in every way. The successful days will turn in to years and subsequently in to a most successful life. A life where you are happy, your goals are achieved and your dreams are fulfilled.

I have also crafted an ideal routine for those who have busy mornings, at the end of the book, that anyone can follow irrespective of the kind of person you are and the work that you do.

wake up

Hope this book helps you make a perfect start to your morning and achieve great heights.

Wishing you a highly successful and productive life!

Signing off from Mumbai,

Aruna Joshi
January 2017

1

WAKE UP AND FOLLOW YOUR DREAMS

1

Well Begun Is Half Done

"Be willing to be a beginner every single morning."
~ Meister Eckhart ~

The beginning is the most important part of any work. Where one begins greatly influences, where one ends. In the movie, "Indiana Jones and the Last Crusade", Indiana was required to find the perceived location of the holy grail. His father had done copious amounts of research dedicated to the discovery of the grail; the cup of Christ. He had journaled his research entirely within one book. His research included a highly-detailed map that gave the precise location of the grail and explicit directions to get there. However, the map was entirely useless to anybody because it was missing one important fact…where to begin. Without an accurate beginning, the remaining details were a struggle to follow and comprehend. So, the start is the critical to any story, including that of your day.

> The morning sun rays and its effusive energy showers the earth with hope and assurance.

Waking up in the morning marks the beginning of a whole new day. The morning sun rays, and its effusive energy showers the earth with hope and assurance. The whole nature rebounds with an invigorating feeling. It brings you another chance to create possibilities, to work towards your dreams, to make a difference in the world, to use your best potential and to explore new horizons.

Irrespective of how hard the previous day may be, each sunrise always brings in new desires, dreams, aspirations, with the hope and confidence to achieve those. Every morning marks a fresh beginning to your life.

There may be days when you 'wakeup from the wrong side of the bed', in a groggy mood, irritable and when nothing seems right. Nothing goes as per your plans, you get unexpected and unpleasant surprises throughout the day; and at the end of the day you label the day as a 'bad day'.

Similarly, there may be days when you wake up cheerful, happy and energetic and you are ready to head start the day. The day goes perfectly as planned. You accomplish a lot of things and even as the day ends you are left with a lot of energy. At the end of the day, you may call that day as one of the most productive and successful days.

What is the differentiator between the two days? It is how you wake up in the morning, and what you do for the first few hours after waking up. As much as we talk about 'waking up from the right side of the bed', the time between waking up and facing the world is also most crucial, as it sets the foundation for the rest of the day. How you think and how you feel undoubtedly sets the tone for the entire day.

Can a bad start of a day be converted in to a good and fruitful day?

Recently, I had this experience, where one disturbing thought could have ruined my entire day. That day I had a writing assignment to be submitted. So, I decided to set everything aside and committedly work on it. As soon as I woke up, I made a cup of my energizing masala tea and locked myself in my study to avoid any of the outside disturbances. I opened my laptop, and while it was booting, I thought of checking my mobile phone. There was some nasty message from a friend, which induced a lot of negativity in me. It was so provoking, that I replied back, and that started a pessimistic conversation. While I was at it something within, told me, "Hey! Do you really want to get into this?" That thought momentarily pulled me out of the conversation. There was a book on positive quotes lying beside me. I randomly opened it and there was a thought that said, "The greatest power a person has is the power to choose." This quote brought a shift in my thoughts.

> How you think and how you feel undoubtedly sets the tone for the entire day.

"Yes!", I decided, "I have the power to choose, and I choose not to entertain any negative thought and engage in any disempowering conversations. I am not going to let anything ruin my entire day." Making this promise to myself, I went down for a walk. This helped me to break the chain of negative thoughts. That 20 minutes of physical activity made me feel good about myself and gain control over my thoughts. I came back fresh, meditated for 10 minutes and got back to my writing assignment and finished it on time.

Had I not broken the spiral of negative thoughts that had started building up, at the right time, it would have robbed me of a peaceful and productive day. I would not have been able to complete my assignment and ended up feeling frustrated and irritated at everyone around. Instead, I ended up having a fruitful and rewarding day, because I chose to start it right.

Everything is in the mind

Even though we have a power to choose, we don't exercise it much. We often get carried away by the incidents that happen in our lives and we lose our power to those situations. At the end of the day we get pushed in a victimized zone and label it as a 'bad day'. The secret lies in being conscious about every thought and choosing them carefully. Thoughts are like seeds, sown in our minds. They could be positive or negative. The ones that we nurture and pay attention to, will grow and manifest. These thoughts ultimately control our being and navigate us through the day. Hence the state of our mind can directly dictate our day.

> Thoughts are like seeds, sown in our minds. They could be positive or negative. The ones that we nurture and pay attention to, will grow and manifest.

The emotions that we go through, also have a direct impact on our physical and mental well-being. If you sleep after a heated argument with your spouse, feeling sad and angry, or after watching a horror movie feeling fearful; it is bound to affect your sleep and there is a sure chance, that you may wake up feeling groggy and heavy. Too much of physical activity in the night or the previous day, leaves you tired, in aches and pains when you wake up in the morning. When you are not up to it physically, it affects your emotional and mental state considerably.

Even if the day has started on a bad note, you just need to change your state of mind to transform it in to a good day. Ultimately, they are just thoughts and feelings that you wake up with. You not only have a choice to change your thoughts, but you also have the power to do so.

It helps to have a routine

Research says that our brain loves efficiency. If we do a certain activity repeatedly, the neurons in the brain naturally align themselves to form a pathway, so that the information can be processed faster. You must have observed that if we do one activity repeatedly over a period of time, it almost happens naturally. It turns into a habit.

> Even if the day has started on a bad note, you just need to change your state of mind to transform it in to a good day.

If you have a set morning rituals that you follow, you don't have to waste time in the morning thinking and worrying about it. Highly successful people have their fixed routines which they strictly follow irrespective of the time and place they are in. This greatly increases their efficiency and productivity. This is an advantage of having a morning routine.

So, how should our mornings look like?

We are all unique souls and have come to this planet with a unique purpose. We are living in different geographical locations, facing different situations, working in different professions, and are from different cultural and religious backgrounds. Hence there cannot be a fixed recipe of a morning routine for everybody. Some may like to start their day with a cup of coffee or tea, while others would spring out of their beds and get straight into some physical activity. Some may want to start their day with a prayer, while others would prefer to finish doing the most difficult task of the day. Whatever way each one of us may choose to start the day, most of the morning activities are similar as we all need to cater to our mind, body, and soul.

Though we are different in various factors, the common aspiration we all have is to be physically fit, mentally healthy, emotionally strong, and socially acceptable. We all want to be happy and successful in life. Most of our goals usually stop short of the first step, be it fitness, nutrition, business, finance, or relationships.

It is said, "Journey of thousand miles begins with a single step."

Taking the first step – the start, is crucial. If we break this journey into several days and head-start each day in an empowering way, we are sure to achieve happiness and success.

> If you have a set morning rituals that you follow, you don't have to waste time in the morning thinking and worrying about it.

Successful people are in the habit of doing this. They follow certain morning rituals; the first things they do before anything else. This not only makes their day productive but also helps them move towards their goals slowly and steadily.

Most successful people tailor make their morning routine, defined by their personality, their nature of work, and their aspirations and goals. For example, a sports person would spend a few hours working out every morning, an actor would use the same time in exercise regime and beauty care, whereas a CEO may utilize the same time for replying to the emails and physical exercise.

A lot of research has been carried out on how successful people carry out their morning routines; as that gives us a glimpse into that part of their life which has majorly contributed to their success.

Here are a few examples,

Steve Jobs, former Apple CEO gave himself a motivational speech every morning. He was responsible for turning Apple into the world's biggest company. He was highly passionate and quality driven. His famous quote, "Your time is limited, so don't waste it living someone else's life. Don't be trapped by dogma - which is living with the results of other people's thinking. Don't let the noise of others' opinions drown out your own inner voice. And most important, have the courage to follow your heart and intuition", gives an insight into the person that he was. He believed in simplicity and focus. To ensure that he got the best out of himself, he drew inspiration from his own self.

After waking up, Steve Jobs would go to the mirror, look at himself and ask: "If today was the last day of my life, would I be happy with what I'm about to do today?" If Jobs found himself saying no to this question too often, he said he knew that something needed to change.

The success of apple has proved that.

What a thoughtful and insightful way of starting the day. By doing this first thing in the morning, he made sure that he was taking each step towards the most successful life.

Ophra Winfry, one of the most powerful celebrities of the world, loves to spend 20 minutes in stillness twice a day. She has seen all the lows that life could possibly offer. She went through child abuse, rapes, early age pregnancy, utter poverty and much more. Another woman in her place would have landed up in a mental asylum. But Ophra has stood tall and strong showing direction and inspiring

wake up

millions. She draws her strength from the 20 minutes she spends in stillness. She says, "this practice induces hope, a sense of contentment, and deep joy. Knowing for sure that even in the daily craziness that bombards us from every direction, there is still the constancy of stillness. Only from that space can you create your best work and your best life." For Ophra, 20 minutes of stillness, leads to a productive and successful day.

Howard Schultz, Starbucks CEO, gets up at around 4:30 a.m. every morning to walk his three dogs. Then after the power walk, he come home and makes coffee for himself and his wife by 5:45 a.m. Schlutz is very particular about the kind of coffee he drinks, using a "coarse grind of aged Sumatra" steeped for 3-4 mins in boiling water, according to BusinessWeek. After that, it's time for work.

Jennifer Aniston, former 'Friends' star is well-known for her gorgeous good looks and youthful glow. She pays special attention to body care, and that shows. Her routine comprises of waking up at 4.30, drinking hot water with lemon, washing her face with soap and water and meditating for 20 minutes. Her breakfast is a protein shake, and then she's off to her personal trainer. 30 minutes of spin, 40 minutes of yoga and then, she goes to the gym. A perfect recipe for a gorgeous body, beautiful skin, and a peaceful mind.

Jeff Bezos, the founder of Amazon, prefers a leisurely morning. He prefers to spend some quality time with his wife and children on the breakfast table. That helps him maintain a healthy work-life balance. He particularly avoids early morning meeting. Spending the morning this way, also keeps him stress-free and spend the day more productively.

Richard Branson, an entrepreneur and founder of Virgin group, wakes up really early. In his blog post, the entrepreneur explained why he wakes up at 5 a.m.: "I'm able to do some exercise and spend time with my family, which puts me in a great mind frame before getting down to business."

Everyone has a typical morning routine – something that they do before doing anything else. This is also the differentiator between the highly successful and not so successful people. Because, how you spend the couple of hours after you wake up can define your productivity and success. However, a common thread can be plucked out from the morning routines of those who have made a mark in their respective ways. This can be used in designing a power packed morning routine.

The common features from the morning routines of the successful people can be listed as below,

- Physical Activity
- Nutritious and Energizing Breakfast
- Practicing Meditation
- Practicing self-Motivating techniques
- Goal Setting and Visualization

To make the morning routine more effective and fruitful we can add certain things like,

- Listening to uplifting music
- Expressing gratitude
- Practicing laughter
- Practicing an art form
- Relaxation Massage

- Saying Affirmations
- Spending time with family

We need to pay as much attention to our emotions, mind and soul as much we pay to our physical body. It is only when our mind, body and soul are in harmony, can we work at our optimum levels.

If you are able to incorporate all these things in your daily morning routine, it will make you 'healthy, wealthy and wise' in its true sense. A perfect recipe for a daily morning routine can be some form of exercise, a healthy breakfast, some form of quiet time, visualization of goals, motivation, garnished with prayer, gratitude, laughter, music, affirmations and so on.

When you start every day with healthy habits and focus on what is important for you in your life, you consciously and subconsciously take actions towards the life you want. The main benefits of a following a morning routine every day is that, not a day goes by when you are not thinking about your goals and your life; which in turn helps you achieve them and live the most productive and successful life. Depending on what your morning routine consists of, it can help you with everything from getting more focused and effective to getting into physical shape.

ARE YOU A MORNING LARK, A NIGHT OWL OR A HUMMING BIRD?

2

Quality Sleep Is Important

"Morning is wonderful. It's only drawback is that it comes at such an inconvenient time of the day."
~ **Glen Cook** ~

Do you resonate with any of these?

You are in a middle of a video conference and you yawn or even doze off. It could turn out to be one of the most embarrassing moments of your life.

You are driving on a highway in the night, sleep overtakes you, and it is impossible for you to drive any further. It could be highly dangerous.

Or there are moments when everybody around you is asleep and you are staring at the blank ceiling unable to sleep. It could be utterly frustrating to be not able to sleep at a desired hour.

It has happened with all of us some time or the other. Imagine if there was no system that governed the sleep and wakefulness in our body, what a mess it could create.

Importance of quality sleep

Sleep is undeniably the most important factor to keep us alert and functional throughout the day. We humans are designed to sleep in the night and work during the day. So sometimes staying up much later than usual and rising a few hours early can be weary. People who do shift duties or travel a lot across different time zones usually face this problem. We all have different sleeping patterns, and it is important to recognize those.

I am a person who can stay awake until late, but find it extremely difficult to wake up early in the morning. There was a time when I was constantly fighting this. People around me made me feel as if I was committing some sin by sleeping till late; especially after marriage when a girl is supposed to fulfil a lot of responsibilities. People advised that I must try and change myself. I couldn't and I felt very guilty about it. I even labelled myself as a 'bad wife.' and a 'bad daughter-in-law'. Instead of accepting the fact, and try to work around it, I always resisted and tried to change. Maybe because I feared rejection. The result was, I was miserable. I was trying hard to sleep early through my most productive and creative time and wake up feeling irritated, craving for more sleep. After years of this fruitless effort, there came a point in my life, when I realized, 'I am a unique person with certain characteristics and I need to accept myself the way I am." This released me from the guilt trap and helped me take charge of my life.

> We all have different sleeping patterns, and it is important to recognize those.

Quality sleep is crucial for our physical and mental well-being. Most of the organs of our body are constantly working; and they need proper rest to rejuvenate and energise. Body has its own mechanism and an innate wisdom to repair and heal itself. This is only possible when it is completely at rest. In children sleep also supports their growth and overall development.

Studies show that a good night's sleep can help you learn anything better, be it a new skill, a language, any subject or any activity. Similarly sleep deficiency can lead to lack of focus and concentration, frustration, depression, stress, and mood swings.

The amount of sleep required by an individual may vary from person to person. However, it is said that an average human being is designed for 16 hours of wakefulness and 8 hours of sleep. Some can do with even 6 hours, while some need a good 10 hours sleep.

> Quality sleep is crucial for our physical and mental well-being.

Scientists say, like all other body functions even our sleep is regulated internally. When you are in a wakeful state for a longer time, some structure in the brain naturally prompts you to sleep. However, the quantity and quality of sleep is governed by a lot of internal and external factors. These could be the food habits, consumption of caffeine, light, stress, ambience, etc.

Our sleeping patterns change with age. As we get older quantity and quality of sleep reduces, hence it becomes difficult to stay awake and also to stay asleep. Just like diet and exercise, a good night's sleep is essential for good health, for keeping alert and energetic, and for building body's defences against infection, chronic illness, and even heart disease.

Most of us have some degree of preference for late night or early mornings. We all have our peak energy work hours and periods of rest. And it differs from person to person. However, we can broadly classify them into three choronotypes. Out of these two are extremes while one falls somewhere in between. The 'early to bed and early to rise' types are the Morning Larks, the 'late to bed and later to rise' types are the Night Owls and then there are those who are ready to buzz any time, early or late are the Humming Birds.

The Night Owl

The Night Owls often wake up late after wrestling with the snooze button for a while. If they are working professionals, they have a tendency to skip the breakfast, and they're always rushing to get to work in the morning. They prefer to do most of the jobs in the evening or late night. You will find them doing things like laundry or surf the Internet at midnight. They dislike early morning activities and enjoy late night parties. They have to really struggle to fulfil any business commitments in the morning such as breakfast meetings. They can best work with flexi timings. Night owls will try to convince you that they're at their most productive after the sun sets, claiming proudly that they worked all night. Their quality of being able to stay awake till late makes them easily cope up with jet lag. Though there is no concrete evidence, studies show that people from creative fields are night owls.

The Morning Lark

The Morning Larks linger over a cup of coffee, and spend time reading the morning paper, simply because they have enough time to do so as they are early risers. They can plan their day in a better way. They are usually disciplined. The early risers get a lot of jobs done before the sun is up each day. They work best in day shifts. They may have difficulty in adjusting with the jet lag. If you ever invite them to a night party, there is a possibility that they would have already cut off from everybody even before the party has begun.

The Humming Bird

The Humming Birds occasionally get up at dawn to go fishing, and sometimes stay up long past your usual bedtime at parties. They are more flexible and can adapt to the situations better.

Whatever chronotype you may belong to, you may have to struggle hard if it does not agree with your working schedule. According to your chronotype, you may have specific time that is your most productive time. Once you figure that out, you can put in your best in whatever you do. Some workplaces in USA have started respecting the biological rhythms and come up with an idea of a flexi schedule. It would be wonderful to work in such a workplace, especially if you are a night owl.

> Whether you are a lark, an owl or a humming bird, you need your quota of sleep to energise and rejuvenate yourself.

Whether you are a lark, an owl or a humming bird, you need your quota of sleep to energise and rejuvenate yourself. It is not mandatory to start the morning really early; but whatever time you wake up, you can start your morning rituals.

Instead of trying hard to change yourself from what you are to what others would like you to be, why not recognize and accept who you are and build your life around it. Doing this, will bring out your best potential and help you live a life of your dreams.

WAKE UP TO FITNESS

3

Humans Are Designed For Movement

~~~~

"Take care of your body,
it's the only space
you have to live in."

~ Anonymous ~

Ever wondered how highly successful people handle their demanding schedules and the stress it entails, so efficiently, without falling prey to any major illnesses? How they are brimming with incredible energy all the time? Well, apart from many things they follow, the most important and indelible part of their morning routines is physical fitness regime.

Wouldn't you feel great if you ran 10km without feeling tired? Wouldn't you feel happy to come back home from a hard day's work and still be energetic to play cricket with your little one? This is only possible when you are physically fit. Maintaining a good level of physical fitness is something that we all aspire for.

But What does being physically fit mean?

According to the United States Department of Health and Human Services, physical fitness is defined as "a set of attributes that people have or achieve, that relates to the ability to perform the physical activity."

A lot has been spoken about the sedentary lifestyle we lead now-a-days and the associated health risks such as obesity, diabetes, Cardio vascular issues and so on. Most of the times you may find yourself either sitting at your desk, working on the computer, or watching television or reading. Though short sessions of sitting are necessary for the body to rest and rejuvenate itself; long hauls of sitting behind the computer screen or on the couch can cause serious damage to your health.

What exactly happens when you are sitting most of the time? Sitting curves your spine as you slouch, putting strain on your spinal cord and ultimately preventing your lungs from getting enough space to expand fully. When your lungs are not breathing in completely, the oxygen supply to all the organs of your body gets depleted. Subsequently there is less oxygen supply to your brain which ultimately leads to loss of focus and concentration. This reiterates the importance of right posture even while sitting.

> **The best time to exercise is in the morning as the energy levels are optimum during that time.**

Have you experienced that when you are doing some creative work sitting in front of the computer, and after a while you turn blank? Your mind is jammed and no fresh ideas come in. On the other hand, when you are walking or doing some physical activity, some brilliant ideas might just pop up. So, when you're sitting, you are probably focusing less, than you are when you were moving around.

I remember an interesting story my school teacher had told about a German philosopher and writer. He was once thinking about a plot for his novel while walking. He was so engrossed that he didn't even realize that by the time he had finished thinking about the whole plot of the story, he had crossed international border!

STRESS - A LIFESTYLE THREAT

Our lifestyle has an enduring effect on our mental and emotional health as well. There is an important factor which has become an integral part of our lifestyle, and that is stress. We face so many stress inducing situations every day. There are challenges at every step; be it health, relationships, money, career, almost in every sector of our life. The timelines to meet, the bills to pay every month, the cut-throat competition, all these things add up to stress and more stress every day. When we are stressed, our body releases stress hormones such as cortisol and alike, to prepare itself to deal with the stressful situations. These stress hormones are nothing but natural steroids that provide instant energy that our body requires to deal with the situation. If these are not metabolized over time, they may result into obesity, decreased bone density, BP, diabetes and many more so called life style diseases.

> It is important to cover all the muscles during the workout.

Although we cannot avoid stress, we can certainly manage it. And one of the ways to do so effectively is by doing some physical activity. Exercise and other physical activities produce endorphins, chemicals in the brain that act as natural painkillers, improve the ability to sleep, which in turn reduces stress.

Research has shown that walks especially in parks and in nature is good for a creative, sharp, and concentrated mind. You may often feel lighter, happier, and more focused the very moment you step outside your home, office, or any closed place into nature. This is because when your body is moving, you are breathing harder and your breath is reaching every cell of your body and the wheels of your mind are turning as well. The nature around adds to a calming effect.

Physical fitness is the most important aspect of our existence, as we as human beings are designed for movement. Moreover, it is our body that will take us through this journey of life. However, most often, we take it for granted most of the times. As we age we fall prey to various lifestyle diseases. This acts like a wakeup call that our body gives us, and at times it is too late to recover health at that time.

FIND WAYS, NOT EXCUSES

What if we start an exercise regime quite early in life? As they say, "Prevention is always better than cure." If we make fitness as integral part of our daily morning routine, we will be saved of much trouble later on. If we miss the exercise regime in the morning we may find numerous excuses in the form of social commitments, tiredness, lack of energy and so on; to not do it in the evening. Hence it is prudent to inculcate some form physical activity in the morning routine. It may not be a full-fledged workout if time doesn't permit, but they can be some simple exercises. Any physical movement is good, after all. A physical activity in the morning pumps in a lot of energy to carry on through the rest of the day. It wakes up your mind to focus better on the jobs in hand.

> It is more important to do the workout than to ponder upon when to do and not do it at all.

When we talk about a physically fit person, what comes to your mind? A weight-lifter, a gymnast, a marathon runner, a sports person or may be a hero proudly showing his six packs. But fitness is more than actually doing these activities. Very simply, it can be defined as the body's ability to function effectively and efficiently, free from diseases and the flexibility to perform any task.

To start with, we need to mark ourselves on the scale of fitness. Once we know where we stand, we can just move further from there. It is mandatory for everyone to engage into some form of physical activity given the sedentary life styles we live. Many people complain that they are not left with much energy to exercise, or they feel very tired after their workouts. Proper nutrition and sleep go hand in hand with physical fitness. If you have not had a six to eight hour of sound sleep or have skipped your meal or are experiencing stress, you will be left with no energy to do the fitness training.

> Your workout should depend on your body type, sleep cycles and it should be supported by nutrition.

To be called as a physically fit person, the following parameters need to be fulfilled,

Cardiovascular / respiratory endurance – The ability of body systems to take in, process, and deliver oxygen to various parts of the body.

Stamina – The ability of body systems to process, deliver, store, and utilize energy.

Strength – The ability of a muscular unit, or combination of muscular units, to apply force.

Flexibility – The ability to maximize the range of motion at a given joint without much trouble.

Power – The ability of a muscular unit, or combination of muscular units, to apply maximum force in minimum time.

Speed – The ability to minimize the time cycle of a repeated movement.

Coordination – The ability to combine several different movement patterns into a singular distinct movement.

Agility – The ability to minimize transition time from one movement pattern to another and perform it with ease.

Balance – The ability to control the placement of the body's center of gravity in relation to its support base.

Accuracy – The ability to control movement in a given direction or at a given intensity perfectly without faltering.

> Muscle tear happens when you do the workout, hence substantial amount of proteins should form an important part of your diet.

If you are able to achieve, all the above through your exercise, then you can be certified as physically fit. Weight loss just happens as a bye-product.

There are various physical activities that can be made a part of your morning routine, and the combination of some can help you pass all the fitness parameters.

BRISK WALK

Walking is the simplest form of physical exercise. You don't need a trainer or any special equipments; and the best part is, it is free, enjoyable and already a part of your life. To get maximum benefit out of it, you just need to do it correctly. If this is done for a longer period, it will melt your pounds, tone your flabs, and leave you feeling good. If you are lucky to have a park or a beach near your house, where you can go for your walks, it can be highly therapeutic.

Brisk walking or Power walking can burn fat quickly and effectively. It gives you the benefit of a run, walk and workout as well. Here is how you do it correctly. Stand straight, with your arms by your sides and pull your navel towards your spine so that your core muscles are working. Focus your eyes five to six meters ahead and keep your shoulders relaxed. Bend your elbows at a 90 degree angle and cup your hands lightly.

> If you have less time during mornings, the least you can do some push-ups, squats, plank or basic crunches or a few yoga asanas that can give a complete stretch to your body.

Starting with the heel, take a step forward with your right foot and move your arms in the opposite direction (i.e. as your left arm moves forward, your right moves back). Repeat the same for the left foot. While doing this, you can count the number of steps and sync your breathing with your steps.

Walking on different terrains like grass, mud, ground, sand or rocky ground have their own benefits. You can try walking on steep slopes and rough terrains. This gives a healthy workout to your muscles and helps you focus better.

Once you get into the routine of walking in the morning, you can be innovative and try out different types of walking and go with the one that suits you the best.

WORKOUT IN THE GYM

Along with maintaining the basic level of physical fitness, if you are also looking at shaping up, and aspiring to have a sculpted body like your favourite film star; working out in the gym can be the best option for you. Gyms have better equipments and space than home. You also get an advantage of working out under the guidance of a professional trainer. Here, you get a chance to work out every muscle and develop a six-pack body. Apart from the health advantages like building muscle strength, balance, flexibility and weight loss, gym becomes a social platform, where you can meet like-minded people who have similar fitness goals and passionate about their health. It can be a positive social experience. Many people feel more committed to do a regular workout because they have paid for it and have company while doing the workouts.

> Body requires essential fats. Half a table spoon of ghee in the morning can provide the required fat percentage.

Some of the basic gym workouts can be,

SQUATS: Squats use the largest muscle group of the body and is good at burning calories. The right way of doing squats is-

- Keep your back straight
- Spread your feet apart so that they are in line with your shoulder
- Keeping your knees over your ankles go downwards as if sitting on a chair
- Come back to the original position and repeat.

LUNGES: Lunges use the same muscle group as squats plus the leg muscles. In addition to burning calories and toning muscles, it also improves balance. The right way of doing lunges is-

- Take a big step forward and bend the knee to 90-degree angle
- Keep your spine in a straight position
- The knee of the trailing leg should come closer to the floor
- The toes should accept significant body weight
- Then return to normal position and repeat with the other leg

CRUNCHES: The standard crunches use the abdominal muscles. It is a good exercise to strengthen and define the abdominal muscles. The right way of doing crunches is-

- Lie on your back with feet flat on the floor
- Let your head rest over your palms
- Press your lower back down
- Contract your abdominal muscles, raise your head, neck and shoulders and upper back in a smooth motion, off the floor.
- Tuck in your chin
- Slowly go back as you came up and repeat

PUSH-UPS: The basic push-up uses the upper body (chest, shoulders, and triceps) and core (abdominal muscles). It strengthens these muscles and is also effective in weight loss and shaping up the body. The right way to do push-ups is-

- Stand straight and spread your arms little more than your shoulder width
- Place your hands firmly on the floor, directly under your shoulders

- Ground your toes into the floor and flatten your back so your entire body is neutral and in straight line
- Bend your elbows and take your chest near the floor
- Then push your body away from the floor until your arms are again fully extended

THE PLANK: The plank is one of the best exercises because it tightens the deepest core muscles. It's a static exercise. The right way of doing the Plank is-

- Start on your hands and knees on the ground. Your hands and knees should be shoulder-width apart.
- Lift your knees off the ground and push your feet back, bringing your body to full extension.
- where you use your arms to raise yourself off the floor and hold the whole body straight and rigid, like a plank of wood.
- Keep your palms directly below your shoulders and pressing against the ground.
- Aim to hold this position for 30-45 seconds

YOGA

Yoga is known to have greater advantages over other form of exercises. It does not need any costly equipments. It can be practiced inside a room or in open air. Hence it is easy to practice throughout the year.

Two main advantages of Yoga are prevention of disorders and ailments and maintenance of health and fitness in daily life. Other advantages include flexible muscles, supple joints, relaxed and tension-free mind and efficiently working vital organs such as the heart, lungs, endocrine glands, liver, pancreas and good balance between various functions, such as neuromuscular coordination, etc.

It would be ideal to do a forty-five minutes to an hour Yoga routine, but even a ten minute of basic asanas will do some good. An important thing while doing yoga stretches is the focus on breathing. Following are the five yoga poses that you can practice first thing in the morning – before anything else.

CHILD'S POSE (BALASANA): This is one of the easiest poses in yoga. However, should not be performed by pregnant women, or person suffering with knee injury or diarrhoea.

Benefits of Balasana

The benefits are many. It straightens and relaxes spine, gently stretches ankles, hips and shoulders. It relieves a person of fatigue and anxiety and induces a sense of calmness. It stimulates digestion and eases back and neck pain.

Step by step guide

- Spread a yoga mat and sit on your heels, your knees together
- Slowly bend forward, touching your forehead to the floor and exhale
- Extend your arms towards the front with your palms facing down
- Now press your chest gently on your knees and regulate your breath for 45 to 60 seconds.
- As you exhale, soften your body and the arms. Repeat for 6-12 breaths.

- Place your palms under the shoulders and gradually raise your upper body to return to the sitting position on the heels while inhaling. Do this very slowly and relax
- Do as many times as you feel comfortable.

CAT/COW POSE (BIDALASANA): It is good to start the yoga practice with this asana.

Benefits of Bidalasan

It helps loosen your body. It relieves your body and relaxes your back and neck.

Step by step guide

- Start with your hands and knees on the floor with knees under your hips and wrists under your shoulders
- Make your back flat and your spine neutral and inhale
- Round your spine towards the ceiling and pull your belly button up towards the spine.
- Tuck your chin towards your chest and let your neck release (This is the cat-like shape)
- On your inhale, arch your back, let your belly relax and go loose.
- Lift your head and tailbone up towards the sky, without putting any unnecessary pressure on your neck (This is the Cow-like pose)
- Continue flowing back and forth from Cat Pose to Cow Pose, and connect your breath to each movement inhale for Cow Pose and exhale on Cat Pose.

- Repeat for at least 10 rounds, or until your spine is warmed up.

STANDING FORWARD BEND POSE (UTTANASANA): Though the benefits of this asana are many, avoid doing it if you have had recent injury or surgery of back, keens, hips or shoulders.

Benefits

In the Standing Forward Bend Yoga posture, your head hangs below the heart allowing fresh oxygen-rich blood to flow to your brain. This rejuvenates and revitalizes cells and provides the complete body a fast boost of oxygen.

Step by step guide

- Stand straight and keep your feet and shoulder distance apart and parallel to each other
- Now breathe out and gently bend down from the hips (not the waist) and place your chest and stomach on your thighs
- Make sure that you don't bend your knees; they should be straight over your toes
- Slowly begin to straighten out your legs but make sure that your chest and abdomen never leave your thighs.
- Now elevate your hips as you straighten through your hamstring muscles all whereas pressing your heels into the ground.
- Once you're feeling stable, cross your forearms, grab your elbows and hang your head down.
- If you're enough flexible, you'll attempt to bring your palms to the ground or hold your heels from behind.

- Begin by holding this pose for thirty seconds and step by step work your way to one minute at a time.
- While holding this position, gently inhale and exhale.
- While breathe in, try to lift and lengthen your torso with each exhalation, try to go deeper and deeper into the stretch.
- There another way to increase the stretch is to roll on to the balls of your feet and lean slightly forward. This stretches the backs of your legs and permits you to carry the pose for extended.
- Don't shut your eyes throughout this Asana.
- Try to hold this pose for 30 seconds.
- Release this pose by placing your hands back on to your hips and with a deep breath in (inhale), extend your back and come up to the initial position.

DOWNWARD DOG POSE (ADHO MUKHA SVANASANA): It is one of the most commonly recommended poses for the beginners. It gently stretches most muscles of your body and make its flexible.

Benefits

Adho Mukha Svanasana strengthens the arms and legs and stretches the muscles of the shoulder and the hamstrings and calves. It helps to get rid of stiffness in the shoulders and lengthens the spine and straightens the legs.

Step by step guide

- Stand with your knees directly below your hips and your hands slightly ahead of your shoulders.

- Spread your palms with your index fingers parallel or slightly turned out, and turn your toes inwards.
- Exhale and lift your knees away from the floor. At first keep your knees slightly bent and your heels lifted away from the floor.
- Lengthen your tailbone away from the back of your pelvis and press it lightly toward the pubis.
- Against this resistance, lift your sitting bones toward the ceiling.
- Then with an exhalation, push your top thighs back and stretch your heels down toward the floor.
- Straighten your knees but be sure not to lock them. Firm your outer thighs and roll the upper thighs inward slightly and narrow the front of your pelvis.
- Firm your outer arms and press the bases of your index fingers actively into the floor.
- From these two points, lift along your inner arms from the wrists to the tops of the shoulders.
- Firm your shoulder blades against your back, then widen them and draw them towards your tailbone. Keep your head between your upper arms and don't let it hang down loosely.

TRIANGLE POSE (TRIKONASANA): This asana stretches the muscles and improve the functions of the body. This is a good exercise for pregnant women.

Benefits

This asana improves the blood flow, strengthens the muscles, and reduces BP, stress and anxiety.

Step by step guide

- Stand by keeping distance between two feet
- While inhaling raise the both hands in the upward direction in such a way that they will be parallel to the ground and palms facing downwards.
- Now bend at right side while exhaling and your left hand facing towards the ceiling and right hand touching your right toe
- Keep your eyes facing towards the ceiling (towards the left palm) and do not bend forward or backward. Pregnant women should take care of her balance. You can take support of a wall or your friend to maintain the balance.
- Keep inhaling deeply and while exhaling relax the body more and more.
- Stay for 1-2 minutes in this posture.
- Now inhale and get back to original position.
- Repeat from bending left side then the right side.

Whatever you are looking for in life be it weight loss, a strong and flexible body, glowing and beautiful skin, peaceful mind or good health, yoga has it on offer. Its benefits are immense as it aims at uniting body mind and soul. When these three things are in harmony, the journey through life becomes calmer, happier and more fulfilling.

Yoga is a complete form of exercise by itself, that can be included in the morning routine. But if you are already going for morning walks or to the gym for workouts, doing some form of yoga asana will give extended benefits. If your morning routine is really tight and you are facing a time crunch, the best thing you can do for yourself is a set of 12

Surya Namaskar. Doing 12 Surya Namaskar at a fast pace can be a good cardio vascular workout and if done at a slow pace, these postures help tone the muscles, it can be relaxing and meditative. Moreover, it makes your body more flexible.

Regular practice of Surya Namaskar offers a lot of interesting benefits for every part of the body. These powerful yoga poses have a great impact on the heart, liver, intestine, stomach, chest, throat, and legs – the whole body from top to bottom. It purifies the blood and improves blood circulation throughout the body and ensures proper functioning of the stomach, bowel, and nerve centres. Practicing Surya Namaskar daily helps balance the three constitutions - Vata, Pitta and Kapha - that the body is made up of.

Surya Namaskar forms an excellent link between warm-ups and intense yoga postures. Start your early morning yoga routine with some warm-up stretches to ease out body stiffness. You can then do a few rounds of Surya Namaskar to help increase body flexibility and also prepare the body to stretch more during the intense yoga posture sequence.

SURYA NAMASKAR

One round of Surya Namaskar consists of 12 yoga poses or asanas.

The 12 postures are:

1. Stand facing the Sun with palms folded and both the thumbs touching the chest.

    Breathing: Inhale while raising the hands and exhale as hands are brought down to chest level.

2. Raise hands upward, with feet firmly on the ground, bend backwards, stretch arms fully.

    Breathing: Inhale.

3. Slowly bend forward, hands touching the earth with respect, head touching the knees.

   Breathing: Exhale

4. Set both hands with the palms down firmly on the ground, pull the left leg backward, raise the head looking at the Sun, full weight resting on the two palm and ten fingers.

   Breathing: Inhale

5. Bring right leg back close to left leg, keeping hands and legs straight, bend the body at the hip forming an arch, just like a mountain, known as 'parvathasan or mountain pose'.

   Breathing: Exhale

6. Stretch yourself fully on the ground in the Saashtanga Namaskar pose (all eight 'anga' or parts of the body on the ground – head, thigh, eyes (sight), mind, word, feet, hands and ears (hearing)). In reality, feet, knees, thighs, chest, forehead touch the ground with the hands stretched out and in folded position, with your mind and thoughts on the full namaskar, then slowly turn the head to the sides first to left and then to right so that each ear touches the ground.

   Breathing: Inhale first and then Exhale fully

7. Slowly raise the head, bend backward as much as possible, hands straight, in the cobra pose.

   Breathing: Inhale

8. Parvathasan – same as Step 5.

   Breathing: Exhale

9. Same as Step 4 with the difference that the right leg is brought forward.

   Breathing: Inhale

10. Same as Step 3

    reathing: Exhale

11. Same as Step 2

    Breathing: Inhale

12. Same as Step 1

    Breathing: Exhale, Inhale and Exhale.

You don't need to be doing yoga regularly in order to practice the Surya Namaskar. If performed correctly, this exercise does not strain or cause injury. If performed in the morning, it relieves stiffness, revitalises your body and refreshes the mind. Do it during the day and it will instantly boost you up, practice it after sunset and it helps you unwind.

One set consists of two rounds of Surya Namaskar, first stretching the right side of your body and then the left side. So, when you do 12 sets of Surya Namaskar, you are completing 12 sets x 2 rounds in each set x 12 yoga poses in each equal to 288 yoga poses within 12 to 15 minutes.

One round of Surya Namaskar burns approximately up to 13.90 calories for an average weighing person. You can now set a target for yourself. You can slowly increase the number of rounds of Surya Namaskar to 108. By the time you reach this number, you will become more toned and fitter.

What could be a better way to start the morning!

AEROBICS

Aerobic exercise makes you sweat, breathe harder, and heart race faster. It strengthens your heart and lungs and trains your cardiovascular system to manage and deliver oxygen more quickly and efficiently throughout your body. Aerobic exercise uses your large muscle groups, is rhythmic in nature, and can be maintained continuously for at least 10 minutes.

> When you are working out, you also need carbs to provide you with the energy required to exercise.

What makes it interesting is, aerobic exercises are usually done with music and in a rhythmic pattern. Aerobics keeps you fit, healthy and energetic all the time. It also mentally relaxes you and induces a feel-good factor.

Some of the aerobic exercises are,

Running: Running is improves health, reduces calories faster, and can be turned in to an enjoyable social event. With different marathons happening around, it could be an enjoyable sport as well!

Swimming: The coolest way to stay fit is swimming. It is a good exercise to all the body muscles, especially back and shoulders and arms. It is one of the safest form of exercises also recommended for pregnant ladies and people with joint issues.

Cycling: Cycling is a combination of exercise, adventure, sport and entertainment. It can be also used as a mode of transport. You can use it to reach your office or enjoy a ride through nature. It induces less pressure on the joints, also giving it exercise it at the same time.

Rowing: Rowing is a low-impact alternative to running or cycling that can improve heart fitness and strengthen the muscles of the upper body, back and abdomen. You can enjoy rowing outdoors by joining a rowing club or hiring a rowboat, or indoors using a rowing machine at the gym or at home.

Rhythmic Cardio Exercises: There are aerobic classes where the cardio is done with a high beat rhythmic music. It improves the cardio vascular health and helps reduce weight.

DANCE

Dance can be one of the most enjoyable, recreational, and healthy was of staying fit. Apart from other health benefits such as weight management, muscle tone, strength, flexibility, and spatial awareness, it is one of best ways of self-expression. The biggest advantage of this exercise is that apart from aiming at physical fitness, you can also learn and master a performing art. Twenty minutes of dance on some good music in the morning can do wonders. Dance works very well on emotional and mental health too. There are various forms of dance which you can practice for physical fitness that include Belly dancing, Hip-hop, Jazz, Zoomba, Salsa, Tap dancing, etc.

SPORTS

Sports is one of the most entertaining ways to stay healthy. The primary requirement for playing a sport is physical fitness. Sports can give a big boost to the amount of physical activity in your life. You can choose individual activities like biking, running, swimming, or hiking. Or, you may want to join a club, for soccer, baseball, basketball, hockey, football or tennis. Other than the physical fitness, sports also brings in right attitude, fighter's spirit, can be entertaining and a possibility of a hobby turning into a profession.

Health benefits can be gained through simple everyday tasks, such as raking leaves, cleaning the house, or walking the dog. Pickup your favourite exercise regime. You can have a combination of few of the above as well. It is not important what exercise you follow as much as it is important to be consistent with it and enjoy doing it. Only when you enjoy something, will you look forward to doing it every morning.

ENERGIZE WITH A SUPERFOOD BREAKFAST

4

Don't Eat Less, Eat Right

"If you're going to
fill your body with rubbish,
you're going to feel rubbish."

~ Calgary Avansino ~

Eating a balanced diet is vital for good health. Food provides proteins, minerals, vitamins, fats and energy to our body to grow and function properly. The food that we eat not only affects us physically but it has a great impact on our mental and emotional well-being. That's why our ancestors advocated eating sattvic food. The Sattvic diet emphasises on lacto-vegetarian ingredients that are fresh, seasonal, and naturally sourced (non-processed). But with the change in life-styles, and the advent of processed foods, our eating habits have changed drastically. We live in an era of fast food and fast life, where our food habits are highly compromised. Gone are the days when we used to savour and enjoy a hearty meal with our family. Nowadays, eating food is as quick as filling petrol in the petrol tank, for our body to function. Many a times we skip meals or indulge in junk food, at the risk of our health in the long run.

> If you don't have a proper breakfast in the morning, we develop a craving for food and end up eating more and eating wrong things.

So, what is the ideal way of starting the morning as far as the nutrition goes? The first thing one should have immediately after waking up is a glass of lukewarm water. Our body is in a fasting mode for almost eight to ten hours. The last meal is the dinner. So the body is at rest after the digestion and absorption system is over. Water is the most neutral thing you can have and it caters to all the organs of the body and also hydrates it. If honey and lemon is added to the lukewarm water, it helps in detoxifying and easy removal of waste from the body. Further addition of ginger, cardamom, cinnamon, pepper or other spices render health benefits. This is a wonder drink, good for all, irrespective of the age, body type or the morning routine. The first thing that you put in your body after a gap of about ten hours is significant.

> Always prefer home-cooked food to processed food.

This is an extremely beneficial habit because of its immense advantages,

- It hydrates your body
- Helps in digestion
- Acts as a natural flush
- Gives a boost to your immune system
- Leads to happier skin

There is a well-known phrase "Breakfast like a King, Lunch like a Prince and Dine like a Pauper"

Undoubtedly breakfast is the most important meal of the day. However, in our busy life-styles that we live, breakfast takes a back seat. Most often we don't have time to sit and peacefully have breakfast in the morning, and we tend to skip it, or eat something really unhealthy.

Breakfast provides the body and brain with fuel after an overnight fast - that's where its name originates, breaking the fast! Without breakfast, you are effectively running on empty tank, like trying to start the car with no petrol.

> **Breakfast is the most important meal of the day. Never skip your breakfast. Have it within an hour after you wake up.**

Apart from providing us with energy, breakfast provides our body with the necessary vitamins, proteins, minerals, and other nutrients that helps us pull through the day. If we don't have these nutrients in the morning, it is less likely that we will have it through the day.

Few more important points why one should not miss the breakfast,

- It is good for waistline, as research shows that people who eat breakfast are less likely to be overweight.
- It restores glucose levels, an essential carbohydrate that is essential for brain function.
- Improves your mood
- Reduces stress levels
- Reduces the craving for food, thus preventing you from over-eating
- Provides sufficient energy to the body to carry out other functions and also the physical exercise.
- It has long term health benefits, reducing the risk of obesity, diabetes, blood pressure, etc.

BE MINDFUL OF WHAT YOU EAT

The food that we intake provides us with energy required by our body to perform the day-to-day functions. Many times, we focus on 'how much we eat' rather than 'what we eat'. In the process, we eat little and skip meals. This is extremely unhealthy putting the body at a greater risk of health issues. By doing this, we may lose weight, but we may also lose health in the process. Hence the importance should be given to what we eat as it is commonly said, 'we are what we eat'.

> Carbs are the best source of energy for the five main organs of your body namely, brain, heart, liver, lungs and kidneys.

When you are on a weight-loss regime, it is said that 70% depends on the diet and 30% depends on the physical exercise. This implies that diet forms the most important part of our day, especially the morning routine.

If you go for a walk or any kind of cardio, the lemon-honey drink is sufficient. But if you have to go for a workout it is essential to have a fruit, after this drink, just before the workout.

The next most important thing in the morning, from diet point of view is the breakfast. If you are not going for exercise in the morning than the breakfast should be had within 35 to 40 minutes of waking up. Our body produces acid which is unutilized during the night, hence some solid intake is necessary soon after we wake up. If we don't eat, the acid starts harming the lining of the stomach.

Ideally the breakfast should comprise of the five food groups. Foods are grouped together because they provide similar amounts of the key nutrients of that food group. For example, the key nutrients of the milk, yogurt, cheese and alternative food groups include calcium and protein, while the fruit group is a good source of vitamins, especially vitamin C.

To meet the nutrient requirements essential for good health, you need to eat a variety from each of the five food groups daily, in the recommended amounts. It is not necessary to eat from each food group at every meal. In fact, in some instances, you only need to eat some of the foods in each food group a couple of times a week.

It is also important to enjoy a variety of foods within each of the Five Food Groups because different foods vary in the amount of the key nutrients that they provide. For example, in the vegetables and legumes food group, orange vegetables such as carrots and pumpkins contain significantly more vitamin A than other vegetables such as white potatoes.

There are five food groups that make a wholesome breakfast and they should be included in the morning breakfast.

Vegetables and legumes/beans

Vegetables, including legumes/beans are nutrient dense, low in kilojoules, and are a good source of minerals and vitamins (such as magnesium, vitamin C and folate) and dietary fibre.

Fruit

For fruits, there is plenty of choice throughout the year. Choosing fruits in season provides better value and better quality. Eating seasonally also adds more variety to your diet throughout the year. And just like with veggies,

> Having a fruit is always better than having a fruit juice.

choosing different coloured fruits increases the variety of nutrients, which can enhance your health.

Grain (cereal) foods, mostly wholegrain and/or high cereal fibre varieties

Grain foods are mostly made from wheat, oats, rice, rye, barley, millet, quinoa and corn. The different grains can be cooked and eaten whole, ground into flour to make a variety of cereal foods like bread, pasta and noodles, or made into ready-to-eat breakfast cereals.

> It is good to have all the seasonal fruits.

Lean meats and poultry, fish, eggs, tofu, nuts and seeds and legumes/beans

Traditionally, the foods from this food group are considered 'protein rich'. More importantly however, this food group also provides a wide variety of other nutrients such as: iodine, iron, zinc, vitamins, especially B12, and essential fatty acids.

Milk, yoghurt cheese and/or alternatives, mostly reduced fat

A wide range of milk and yoghurt products are available with varying levels of fat. Milk can be fresh, dried, or evaporated. Cheese is usually high in kilojoules, saturated fat and salt and is best limited to 2-3 times a week. However, some cheeses also have reduced levels of fat and salt.

These five groups of food have to be supplemented by the sixth most important group i.e fluids which include water, coconut water, buttermilk, juices etc. However ideally one should consume 10 -12 glasses of water every day.

So a wholesome breakfast should cover all the six groups.

Some Energising Smoothie Recipes

Smoothies are gaining popularity these days. A smoothie with heavily loaded nutrients can also replace a meal. It can be had anytime of the day; however, the best recommended time is to have it before anything else. Smoothie is easy to make. You just have to blend all the ingredients in a mixer and pour it in a glass and have it.

> Potato with skin is loaded with nutrition and an ideal thing to have before the workout. The way we cook potato with lot of oil is wrong. Don't have it in night.

Listed below are some of the healthy recipes for smoothie and breakfast. The recipes are for one serving.

Banana Strawberry Smoothie

1 small fresh sliced banana + 2 sliced strawberries + 1 cup plain organic soy milk + ¼ cup mint leaves + ¼ cup raw cashews (soaked overnight) + ⅓ cup tofu + ¼ tsp vanilla extract

Humble Bottle Gourd Smoothie

6 inch peeled and sliced Bottle gourd + ½ Lemon + 1cup fresh mint leaves + 1 inch ginger + 2 teaspoons honey

Fiery Red Smoothie

1 chopped apple + 1 chopped carrot + ½ chopped Beetroot + 2 tsp honey + 4-6 ice cubes + coriander for garnish + Sprinkle Black salt and pepper

Fresh Green Smoothie

2 cup chopped spinach + 1 cup chopped pineapple + I chopped carrot + ½ fresh mint leaves + I spoon chia seeds

Some Energising Breakfast Ideas

Some simple Indian Vegetarian Breakfast ideas that have been time tested are as follows:

1. Veg Poha – Either add sprouts or accompany it with any milk product
2. Veg Upma – Make in buttermilk instead of water
3. Veg Oats/Dalia – can be had in association with milk, sprouts or nuts
4. Veg Roti – Grated vegetables with mix flour served with milk or curd
5. Veg Wrap - with paneer/sprouts and grated vegetables
6. Mix dal Cheelas – can be had with mix vegetables
7. Idli- with sambhar made with vegetables and chutney
8. Rava dosa/ Nachni dosa/ Rava uttapa – with sambhar and chutney
9. Thalipith – added with chopped vegetables and curd
10. Veg idli/ dahi idli
11. Sprouts, corn and pomegranate
12. Humus and veggies wrap
13. Mexican beans and 2 toasts

Indian Non-Vegetarian Breakfast

1. Eggs in any form (boiled, omelette, bhurji) with 2 toasts/ chapatti
2. Chicken Sandwich

Continental Breakfast

1. Muesli with milk and nuts
2. Yoghurt with cereals and fruit/nuts
3. Any of the smoothies

The above are the regular recipes, healthy and straight from grandmom's kitchen. But sometimes if you need a change and also want to stay healthy, here are a few recipes that I have tried and would recommend personally.

Oats Upma

Ingredients:

1 carrot, 1onion, 1 potato, 100gms green peas, 100 cauliflower, ½ lemon or ½ cup curd, ½ inch ginger, 1 green chille, oil, grated coconut, coriander, salt, 100gm oats.

Procedure:

Chop all the veggies. Wash and drain out the water and add finely chopped ginger to it. Pour 1tsp oil in a pan.

> It is good to have 2 teaspoons of oil and 2 teaspoons of cow's ghee or white butter every day

Add finely chopped green chilly. Then add all the veggies and sauté. Add oats to it. Sauté again; then add salt to taste and squeeze half a lemon or add curd. Add water and let it cook for 7 minutes. Garnish it further with grated coconut and finely chopped coriander.

Wheat Dosa

Ingredients:

1/2 glass Butter milk, 2 tsp wheat flour, 1 small spoon cumin seeds, salt, 1 green chilly.

Procedure:

Take buttermilk in a container, add wheat flour, cumin seeds, finely chopped green chilly and salt to taste. Bled the batter well. The consistency should be like dosa batter. Take a non-stick pan. Heat it and apply oil. Pour the batter and put the lid. Let it cook on simmer. Apply oil on top and turn it over when it turns crisp. Have it with any chutney or tomato ketchup.

> Anything that nature has given us is not bad.

Oats Rava Dosa

Ingredients:

½ cup oats powder, ½ cup rava, ½ cup curd, salt, ginger-chilli paste

Procedure:

Grind oats to fine powder, add rava, curd, salt, ginger-chilli paste and mix well. Rava and oats should be in equal proportion. Add water to make it into a dosa batter consistency. Soak it for 4-5 hours. Take a non-stick pan. Heat it and apply oil. Pour the batter and put the lid. Let it cook on simmer. Apply oil on top and turn it over when it turns crisp. Have it with any chutney or tomato ketchup.

Rawa Dhokla

Ingredients:

1 cup Rawa, 1 cup curd, garlic-chilli-ginger paste, salt, Eno salt

Procedure:

Make a semi-thick batter of rawa and curd. Add salt to taste, garlic-chilli-ginger paste and let it rest for 4-5 hours. Add a pinch of Eno salt just before making it. Oil a utensil and pour the batter into it. Steam it in the dhokla maker. You can garnish it with coriander and a 'tadka' of oil with cumin seed, sesame seeds and mustard seeds. You can have it as it is or with some chutney.

Due to the change in our lifestyles we have started eating outside frequently and compensate on calories as compared to the home food, which is healthier. In the bargain, we are harming ourselves in two ways. One by eat outside and second by not eating the good food available at home. To follow a healthy diet what one requires is discipline and commitment towards oneself.

5

MEDITATE AND RELAX

5

Quiet The Mind And The Soul Will Speak

"Meditation can reintroduce you to the part that is missing."

~ Russel Simmons ~

Many years ago, meditation was considered as a spiritual/esoteric practice, meant for the saints. But in today's world when science and research has proved the immense benefits meditation has on mind and body, meditation is gaining popularity.

Meditation is not a technique but a way of life. It describes a state of consciousness, when the mind is free of scattered thoughts and various patterns. The observer (one who is doing meditation) realizes that all the activity of the mind is reduced to one. The aim is to reach the thoughtlessness state and touch the inner core.

Meditation is a means of transforming the mind. Regular practice of meditation develops concentration, clarity, emotional positivity, and a calm, seeing of the true nature of things. By engaging with a particular meditation practice, you learn the patterns and habits of your mind, and the practice offers a means to cultivate new, more positive ways of being. With regular work and patience these nourishing, focused states of mind can deepen into profoundly peaceful and energised

> **Meditating regularly can introduce you to the deeper and unexplored side of you.**

states of mind. Such experiences can have a transformative effect and can lead to a new understanding of life.

Meditation is a technique to rest our mind and reach the inner core of our consciousness, by fathoming all the layers covering the core. It is an altered state of consciousness which is different from the normal wakeful state.

During our formal education, the main focus is laid on the external world and very little of mind is cultivated. Therefore, we remain strangers to ourselves, while trying to get to everything else around us. This lack of self-understanding is one of the main reasons for our relationships issues, and for the confusion and disappointment to prevail in our life.

The vast realms of the unconscious mind which is the reservoir of all the experiences, knowledge, wisdom and potential thus remains untapped. Meditation gives you an access to all these. It not only lets you explore the inner world but also helps you gain control over your mind. Regular practice of meditation brings in clarity in thinking, and garner positive thoughts. It helps you focus better on your goals with awareness. Meditation makes you experience a state of bliss, happiness and peace, which is not dependent on the external factors.

> If you are completely present in the moment and enjoying what you are doing, then anything mundane can become a meditation.

Meditation not only benefits at an emotional and psychological level, but helps tremendously on a physical level. A team led by Harvard-affiliated researchers at Massachusetts General Hospital reported these results in the first study "to document meditation-produced changes over time in the brain's gray matter." They observed measurable changes in brain regions associated with memory, sense of self, empathy, and stress start to appear in subjects who practice mindfulness meditation for only eight weeks.

How to meditate? Our mind is constantly thinking and restless by nature. We often jump from one thought to another. At any given point in time our mind is crowded with thoughts. They just come and go, resting for a while. Our mind is just an observer. When we shift our mind's attention from our thoughts, we can reach the thoughtless stage which we can call a meditative stage.

> Make meditation enjoyable. We do only those things on a consistent basis, which we enjoy.

The best time to meditate is in the wee hours of morning. Making it a part of your morning routine will put you in a regular habit of meditating every day. Meditation is not time bound but for practical purposes you can meditate for 20 minutes every day.

If you are a beginner, you can follow the following steps to get into the habit of meditation

1. **Find a quiet place**: Find a place in your house, which is quiet and there is no disturbance. This can be your meditation corner. It should be clean and peaceful. To make it more sacred you can light a candle or keep some flowers for a soothing aroma.

2. **Posture**: Though traditionally people used to sit in lotus posture to meditate, it is not mandatory. It is important to be relaxed during meditation.

Depending on your comfort level, you can either sit down on a mat or on the chair. You just need to make sure that your posture is erect so that you can breathe fully. The position of the arms should be relaxed by keeping the palms facing up in the lap, one over the other, or the hands should be on the knees with palm up or down but fingers loose and relaxed. If sitting in a chair, the feet should be together on the floor, with equal weight.

3. **Beginning** to Meditate: When you relax yourself and close your eyes, your mind will be inflicted with lots of thoughts. If you decide that you are not going to think any thoughts, they will come with double force. That's the nature of mind. The best way to deal with this is let the thoughts come and pass by; don't resist. Just be an observer of those thoughts. Slowly with practice the number of thoughts will reduce and a stage will come when you will experience thoughtlessness. That is the state you need to reach.

4. **Actual Meditation**: Focus on the breath and be one with it. There are three guided meditation given below that might help.

3 SIMPLE MORNING MEDITATIONS

Given below are three simple, but highly effective techniques of meditation. You may incorporate anyone of them in your morning routine.

Being with your Breath Meditation

Find a simple, uncluttered and quiet place where you will not be disturbed. You may sit on the floor with a cushion under you or in a firm chair, with your back straight and your eyes closed. Relax all the Muscles of your body one by one, starting from your toes to your head. Let go of all the tension in your body and relax. Once your body is completely relaxed, focus on your breathing. Observe, as the breath goes in through the nostrils, reaches the depth of your lungs and comes out again through the nostrils. Observe the breath all the way as it touches each part of the wind pipe and then feeling it entering various parts of the lungs. If the breath is deep and slow, that helps. Observe the dry, cold air as it enters the nose when we inhale, and the moist, warm air coming out of the nose. Observe each detail, the temperature, the texture, the fragrance, the length of time of each breath, the feeling of expansion and contraction of diaphragm. you can do this for any number of breaths. Or you may time it. Open your eyes after you reach a peaceful state. This process of conscious breathing really helps if we are agitated, emotionally disturbed or stressed out.

> Pay attention to how you feel after meditating. That will act as a booster for practicing next time.

Gravitational Pull Meditation

Lie down on a bed, couch, or sun lounge or an easy chair, or pile the empty bath tub with pillows and soft blankets. Close both eyes and do nothing. Keeping a smile on the lips helps. Just let go… thinking that the gravitational pull of the earth has completely taken over. As if it's a free fall. Maybe you'll fall asleep. That's fine… Maybe you'll have an inspirational thought. That's fine as well… Maybe you'll just happily float along. Putting on soothing music of our choice really helps

in this process. You can even think that the music is entering the core or the heart as it plays. There is no time limit to this process. Sometimes, not doing a thing, can really sort out many things or issues bothering you.

Letting Go Meditation

Sometimes just letting go after an exhaustive routine is a very effective way to reach our inner self. Try to do anything which is energy consuming, it could be aerobics, skipping, cycling, jumping at one place, fast dancing, or just anything which makes the heart race and breathing fast. Do this for about five to ten minutes. While doing this, it is good to let go of all inhibitions and just enjoy the whole act. Any fast dance number or aerobics music makes this more enjoyable.

> Set aside a few minutes in your morning routine, for visualizing the short term and long term goals you have set for your selves. This will help them become a reality.

At any point when you feel you have done enough, just sit or lie down and let go completely. Feel that the whole body is filled with energy. Just observe and do nothing, while letting go. You can stay like this as long as one can. Feel the whole body and mind refreshed after this process. This can be practiced at any time and place, but it's better to choose a place where one feels comfortable and preferably with no disturbance.

Most of the successful people practice meditation in some form or the other. "When you lose touch with inner stillness, you lose touch with yourself, when you lose touch with yourself, you lose yourself in the world." Says Eckhart Tolle. To make your mark in the world, and to be successful and productive you need to connect to your inner core which is the reservoir of strength and draw energy from there to achieve your goals. Regular practice of meditation helps you achieve that.

VISUALIZE
THE
DAY
AHEAD

6

Get, Set, Goals

~~~~

"Visualize this thing that you want, see it, feel it, believe in it. Make your mental blue print, and begin to build."

~ Robert Collier ~

One thing all the successful people do is, visualize. Before they step into the chaotic world, they visualize their entire day, set the goals for the day and eventually achieve most of them.

How does visualization work?

The first step to success in life is setting goals. It could be losing weight, getting promotion, starting your own business, buying a house, buying a new car, it could be just anything. Setting a goal and writing it down gives a purpose and direction to life. It makes your destination clear, then, it's all about reaching there.

Aristotle said, "First, have a definite, clear, practical ideal; a goal, an objective. Second, have the necessary means to achieve your ends: wisdom, money, materials, and methods. Third, adjust all your means to that end."

Most of us get stuck at the goal stage. Setting goals is easy but following them to the stage of achieving, takes effort. Our negative beliefs, insecurities, fears, doubts, laziness act as hurdles, preventing us from achieving our goals.

What if we are able to see our goals achieved even before we set to achieve them? This is possible through visualization; which is simply a technique for creating a mental image of a future event. When we visualize our desired outcome, we begin to "see" the possibility of achieving it. By doing this, positive feelings are generated within us, which motivates us to take necessary action to achieve those.

Visualization is a proven method to enhance performance supported by substantial scientific evidence. It is used by successful people across a range of fields.

Arnold Schwarzenegger is said to be a firm believer in the power of visualization. He first used it to reach his bodybuilding goals.

> When we visualize our desired outcome, we begin to "see" the possibility of achieving it.

"I had this fixed idea of growing a body like Reg Park's. The model was there in my mind; I only had to grow enough to fill it," he explained. "The more I focused in on this image and worked and grew, the more I saw it was real and possible for me to be like him."

Later, when he changed his career to acting and then politics, Schwarzenegger said he employed similar mental tricks: "It's the same process I used in bodybuilding. What you do is create a vision of who you want to be — and then live that picture as if it were already true."

Michael Phelps who is the 19 times record setting, Olympic medal winner, out of which 15 are gold, gives the credit of his success to the visualization practice. He was practicing this since he was seven years old. Every night before going to sleep he would visualize his perfect swim, each and every stroke in detail and go to sleep feeling victorious, even before the actual swim.

Michael Jordan, the famous Basketball player said "Every time I feel tired while exercising and training, I close my eyes to see that picture, to see that list with my name. This usually motivates me to work again."

Muhammed Ali, the famous boxer said "Champions aren't made in gyms. Champions are made from something they have deep inside them – a desire, a dream, a vision. They have to have the skill, and the will. But the will must be stronger than the skill. To be a champion you must believe you are the best. If you're not, pretend you are."

> Visualization is a proven method to enhance performance supported by substantial scientific evidence.

Various studies in the field have shown visualization affects the cognitive processes in the brain such as motor control, attention, perception, planning and memory. So when you visualize, your brain gets trained for actual performance. It has been found that mental practices enhances confidence, efficiency, and performance all necessary to achieve the best and be successful in life.

Research shows that visualization increases performance by improving motivation, co-ordination and concentration. It also aids in relaxation and helps reduce fear and anxiety. The power of visualization is available to everybody, and it can be done for anything you desire for in your life.

Visualization involves three steps,

1. Envisioning the final outcome of your goal
2. Creating a mental imagery of each step in detail

3. Infusing it with emotions and feelings

For example, you wish to go on a foreign holiday.

First step is to decide your destination – your goal. Second step is to break it down into various steps and create a vivid picture in your mental imagery; such as deciding the dates, the airlines, visa, itinerary, packing, boarding the flight, reaching there and so on. Add further details like what kind of clothes you would be wearing, who will be accompanying you, how you reach the airport, your seat in the aircraft, each and every small detail to the extent you can imagine. Now infuse this imagery with emotions, experience the joy you feel after having achieved what you had aimed for.

> Research shows that visualization increases performance by improving motivation, co-ordination and concentration. It also aids in relaxation and helps reduce fear and anxiety.

When you do this exercise, your mind starts believing it to be true and easily achievable. This sets open the path to actually achieving your goal.

If you can include this practice of visualization in your morning routine, you are sure to have a successful and productive day ahead as it is already a reality in your mind.

Set aside 10 minutes of your time in the morning before anything else. The process is as follows,

Take a paper and a pen and write down the things you would like to accomplish during the day.

Sit in a comfortable posture and close your eyes.

Focus on your breath. Observe your breath as it goes in and comes out. Do this for at least 20 breaths.

Shift your focus to all the parts of your body starting from toe to your head. As you take your attention to various parts of your body, relax them, feel them totally relaxing.

Once you have relaxed your whole body, bring in a white screen in front of your mind's eye (visualize a projector screen). Project the goals you want to achieve through the day. It should run like a movie. Visualize how you would spend the entire day and achieve your goals for the day.

To add a power dose to your visualization process, affirm your desired outcomes. For example, if you have an important meeting during the day, affirm, 'My meeting is highly successful and I have got the contract.' Feel happy and satisfied and do a mental handshake with that person.

Once you are done, open your eyes and head start the day.

WAKE UP WITH A BOOSTER DOSE OF MOTIVATION

7

Your Only Limit Is You

"People often say that motivation doesn't last. Well, neither does bathing – that's why we recommend it daily."

~ Zig Ziglar ~

Imagine the following situations-

Situation 1

You are planning to start an exercise regime; and every morning when you are in bed, you think, "I should start my morning walks", and then you tell yourself, "You need some more sleep, maybe you can start from tomorrow." And then you promise yourself to start from the next day and go back to sleep.

Situation 2

You are working very hard towards your goal; but you encounter failure several times. You start doubting yourself and your capabilities. You may even think of quitting or go into depression.

In both the above situations what you actually need is a slight push – some motivation to move ahead. Because if you do not have motivation, you cannot go very far. Motivation provides a drive to accomplish the set goals, to fulfill responsibilities and to live life to its fullest.

All the successful people also need motivation from time to time, and they draw it from various things around them. It could be a quote by somebody, or some speech, or past achievement – it's different for different people.

Here is an interesting story of Lance Armstrong. At the age of 25, he was diagnosed with advanced testicular cancer in which there is less than 40 percent chance of recovery. Tumors were discovered in his lungs and stomach along with multiple lesions on the brain. Everyone thought that his biking career was over. But Lance Armstrong did not think so.

He was not a person who wouldn't easily give up. He had tremendous faith in himself. But the journey was not easy. One of the first things that he did was to acknowledge the disease that he was suffering from and learn everything he could about it. He read a lot of books, and found help in support groups with people going through similar difficulties.

> To motivate yourself, you can put post-its of positive messages on your mirror or fridge or wherever you see it frequently.

The fight was tough and whenever he felt demotivated, he sought strength and motivation from what his mother Linda Walling had instilled in him.

"Make every obstacle an opportunity",

"Always work hard and good things will happen"

and "Don't believe it when other people say you can't".

His first comeback after beating cancer was not a success in terms of winning a medal as he finished fourteenth in the race. But given the situation he came from, he was hugely successful. He was discouraged and even thought about retirement but constant support and motivation from his fiancée, mother and buddy Chris Carmichael soon had him training for his next race in the Appalachians. He returned from his training a transformed man and never let the constant difficulties plough him down again.

Reading such a motivational story itself motivates you. However, you can find various ways through which you can stay motivated all the time.

Some of them could be as below-

Read a motivational book:

'Books are the best friends', they say. And what could be a better buddy than a motivational book. A good motivational book is that which touches your core, instils positivity in you, brings shift in your thinking, and inspires you to take the step towards your goal. Reading a couple of pages from a motivational book before anything else in the morning can give you the mental strength to go through the day.

> Light candles instead of the tube light. The flickering flame has something hypnotic and healing about it.

Listen to speeches by successful people or watch videos:

Our mind is trained in a particular way since childhood. We form certain beliefs as a result, and live by them. But as we grow, we may realize that certain beliefs are hurdles in the path to success. They pull us back, and stop us from being successful. At such times, we need guidance and motivation to follow the path to success. The best way could be listening to or watching motivational speeches from the people who are already there.

Listen to good music:

Research shows that music has a therapeutic value and has a great impact on the emotional, mental and also the physical state of a person. You can set aside some part of your morning time to listen to the music of your choice – that which peps you up and motivates you or calms you down if you need to. You can also combine it with your physical activity or breakfast.

> Always carry a couple of inspirational books wherever you go. They are the best company you can have.

Read a motivational quote:

Get into the habit of reading a motivational quote everyday. You may write it on a paper and paste it on the mirror or the place where you can always see it. You can also find some on the internet.

Remember all your past achievements:

When you are feeling low, the best thing to do is superimpose it with the feeling of how you felt when you achieved something in the past. It instantly changes the state of mind and leaves you feeling more encouraged and happy about yourself.

Remember all your good deeds from the past:

As humans, we have an innate need to do good to others. It gives us a high when we are able to help others in need. Apparently, it also has an effect on our being. Replaying the good deeds you did in your mind, will motivate you to stay positive and do further good.

Remember all the compliments you received in the past:

Sometimes when we feel low, we are too harsh on ourselves. At such times, it is best to remember the compliments you received from people. It drives away the low feeling and makes you feel good about yourself again.

Express gratitude:

People who regularly practice gratitude by taking time to notice and reflect upon the things they're thankful for, experience more positive emotions, feel more alive, sleep better, express more compassion and kindness, and even have stronger immune systems. Why not make this a morning ritual? Seriously, we have endless number of things to be grateful for!

Appreciate people around you:

William James, well-known psychologist and philosopher, said, "The deepest principle of human nature is a craving to be appreciated." When you give people a sincere compliment, words of encouragement or just a warm smile, you are making their world a better place. You are making them feel appreciated and valuable. This in turn will make you feel same.

> Nurture relationships that will motivate you when you need it the most.

Do what you love:

If you're doing what you love for your living then you don't work a single day. But if you are not, you must do something that you are really passionate about everyday. It could be any art or sport or writing or reading or anything that is very close to your heart. Make it a part of your morning routine.

Talk to your mentor:

Each one of us has a mentor – a person who we look up to for guidance, motivation and inspiration. Mentor is a person who will not be judgmental of you or your actions. He or she will always motivate you to bring out the best in you. A mentor could be your friend, parent, sibling, teacher or any person whom you completely trust, love and respect. Whenever you are feeling low, pick up the phone and talk to your mentor, don't hesitate.

Laugh it out:

Laughing out loud instantly changes the state of mind. In today's times, we have forgotten to laugh. We spent most of our time on social media, where, even if we share or read a joke, our response is 'LOL' or a laughing smiley. Practice laughing out loud. Laughter is indeed the best medicine.

Sing peppy numbers:

This is another way of bringing back the motivation. Sing some peppy numbers loudly. Even if you are not a singer, you can certainly be a good bathroom singer. Don't be conscious about your voice or tune. If you are shy you can go to the bathroom. Try this out, it really works.

Spend time with plants:

Plants not only make your environment pure but they also have a healing effect. Tending to plants can uplift your mood. If they are flowery plants, then the aroma and the beauty of flowers additionally help.

Stop Thinking too much:

Most of the times, we become miserable because we think too much – and these thoughts are usually about the past which has already gone or future which is yet to come. Whereas the reality is only the 'present moment' that we have. Bringing your focus to

> Start your morning with a motivational quote that leaves you feeling positive throughout the day.

the present moment can motivate you to put in your best in that moment without any burden. The best way to do this is focus on your breath.

Following any of the above, or finding your own tools will you afloat even during the storm in your life. When your mind is abuzz with positivity, you attract only positive people and situations in life that help you succeed.

MUSIC IS THE MEDICINE FOR MIND

8

Integrate Music In Your Life

"Music washes away from the soul the dust of everyday life"
~ Berthold Auerbach ~

Have you experienced how music changes your mood? A particular piece of music can make you feel happy, sad, energetic or relaxed. If it can impact the mood, it can also impact the physical, mental and emotional well-being of a person. It has the capacity to chase your blues away and make you exuberant. Music is a natural anti-depressant.

Our association with music go back to the time when we are born. The lullabies sung by our mother took us to the fairy land, putting us to a sound sleep; the jingles we sang in the schools made us happy; then as we aged further, our association with music grew with the movie songs, the music beats, the religious recitations, the party music, the calming music and so on. We have also experienced how each kind of music has had an effect on our mind.

> Our association with music go back to the time when we are born.

In Chinese medical theory, the five internal organ and meridian systems are believed to have corresponding musical tones, which are used to encourage healing. In Indian philosophy we have various ragas associated with the seven major chakras (energy centers) of the body.

Different type of music creates different effects. For example, classical music has been found to cause comfort and relaxation while rock music may lead to discomfort.

> Music undeniably has a definite impact on your mind and mood and subsequently your feelings

Research shows that soothing tunes foster the release of serotonin, a hormone that fosters happiness and a general sense of well-being. It also flushes the body with dopamine, a neurotransmitter that makes you feel good. Music also paves the way for the release of norepinephrine, a hormone that brings about euphoria and elation.

If you feel anxious you naturally want to listen to some soothing music to calm you down, if you are in a romantic mood, say Gazals or some romantic songs create that ambience for you, or if you are in a party mood, you prefer to listen to some peppy music that makes your body vibrate naturally.

All in all, music, undeniably has a definite impact on your mind and mood and subsequently your feelings. For most people, music forms an important part of their life.

People listen to music while commuting, cooking, during their exercise regime or doing any kind of mundane work. But above all music has a therapeutic value.

Music is not only an art, entertainment and pleasure but also acts as a medicine for mind, body and soul. It has been an intrinsic part of all cultures. Research says that it is one of the few activities that involves using the whole brain. Listening to music has immense benefits, few of which are improving memory and focusing attention, for physical coordination and development. Music causes the body to release endorphins to counteract pain as well.

Not all types of music have favourable effects. Music can be distracting if it's too loud or too jarring, or if it competes for our attention with what we're trying to do. This kind of music also has a reverse effect on our being. It can leave us irritable. Negative effects of music on the brain include a reduced ability to concentrate and memorize information. People may also experience agitation or other negative emotions when they listen to music that they do not enjoy.

Our brains are wired to respond to music. Small children start humming and dancing to the music. Mothers across cultures, and throughout time have used lullabies and rhythmic rocking to calm crying babies and put them to sleep. Music increases the concentration and it easily accesses our emotions. Do you remember the nursery rhymes which you were taught as toddlers? You may forget other things that are taught to you but something which has a rhythm to it cannot be easily forgotten. When you

> Listening to music has immense benefits, few of which are improving memory and focusing attention, for physical coordination and development.

hear a song on a radio aren't you immediately transported to a certain place, a specific time in your life, or remember a particular person? After smell, music is second for its ability to stimulate our memory in a very powerful way.

A 2013 study in the Journal of Positive Psychology found that people who listened to upbeat music could improve their moods and boost their happiness in just two weeks.

wake up

In the study, participants were instructed to try to improve their mood, but they only succeeded when they listened to the upbeat music as opposed to the sadder tunes.

And a happier mood brings benefits beyond feeling good.

Given the high therapeutic value of music and its ability to penetrate and touch your heart; how about making it a part of your daily morning routine. You don't really have to set a specific time aside for it. You can listen to music while you are cooking, eating, driving, having breakfast, meditation, exercise or while doing any regular activity. Music only enhances the experience of that particular activity. Music can be a thread woven in the fabric of morning routine.

HAVE AN ATTITUDE OF GRATITUDE

9

Thankful People Are Always Happy

"That breath that you just took...that's a gift"
~ RobBell ~

Saying "Thank You", may be a mechanical act for most of us; but if you know the science and significance behind it, I am sure you will use it more frequently with greater understanding and awareness. Research says, that by acknowledging the goodness in others and for the gifts that the universe bestows upon us, you are benefitted in multiple ways.

- You naturally become happier by counting your blessings
- It reduces the stress and anxiety
- You can sleep better, hence wake up fresh in the morning
- It increases the compassion in us
- It helps us come out of the traumatic situations easily
- It strengthens relationships
- You start to value each and every thing in your life
- It turns you into a positive and optimistic person

Expressing gratitude is the least that you can do for yourselves. Most of the times, we just take things for granted in our life.

For example, if our parents or children do something for us, we feel, it's their duty and we take them for granted.

However, if you start expressing gratitude to not only your near and dear ones, but to people around you, and to the universe, your life will change phenomenally and this world will to seem be a wonderful place to exist.

Gratitude is nothing but noticing small and simple things in life, acknowledging them, being happy for them being a part of your life. Gratitude is about counting your blessings. This practice helps you live out of abundance than out of lack.

> Expressing gratitude is the least that you can do for yourselves.

It completely changes your focus in life from negative to positive making you more happy, strong and resilient. Practicing gratitude makes you look at life as if it were a miracle. Isn't it a miracle that you are educated, had enough money to buy this book and have a pair of perfect and beautiful eyes, and the time and inclination to read this book? This itself is a good enough reason to be grateful for!

If this habit of looking at small wonders in life with grateful eyes is cultivated, you will attract only abundance in your life.

Why not make gratitude a part of your morning routine? What could be a more powerful start to your day. The best part is that you don't even need to set aside a particular time for doing this. When you wake up, thank the universe that you are alive. As you get ready, be grateful that you have the water flowing right into your bathroom, for the aromatic soaps you use, for the beautiful clothes you wear and so on. When you have your breakfast think about how the finished product has reached on your plate. Thank each one involved in the process, so that you could have your favourite breakfast. Thank the farmer, thank the vegetable and the fruit vendor and the person who has cooked the breakfast and thank the universe for the wonderful system that has made it possible for the food to reach on your plate.

> Gratitude is nothing but noticing small and simple things in life, acknowledging them, being happy for them being a part of your life.

There can be numerous reasons for you to be grateful for. What is required is increasing your awareness and sensitivity. You need to be conscious every moment, only then you will notice even the smallest things to be grateful for, in your life. This will make you humble and turn you into a more positive and a happier person.

Gratitude can be cultivated in your life through the following ways:

- **Tune into the positive things/incidences in your life.** This is one of the things that I practice. If I am dreadful about the current situations in my life, I sit and recollect previous such incidences and how I safely came out of those. This makes me feel highly grateful towards the universe /God and reiterates my faith. This exercise helps a lot, particularly during the low phase of life when everything seems to be dark. Remembering positive things and being grateful for them has the power to pull you out of this phase instantly.

- **Write a gratitude letter.** Some of us may not be as good at expressing our feelings upfront, as others. You can pour down your feelings and gratitude in the form of a letter or an email to the people, you feel really grateful about and to those who have contributed to your life's journey. This helps in strengthening the relationships. I do this as a ritual in the last week of December every year. I make a list of people around me who have touched my life in some way. I write to them expressing my gratitude for making my life better. I not only get an encouraging reply but I have also made some strong bonds.

- **Maintain a gratitude journal.** If you are able to carve out even five minutes in the morning, you can list down at least five things that you are grateful for in your life in the journal. There are many more things to be grateful for, but you can start with five and increase the count.

- **Be sensitive and see the intention.** When you receive a gift or someone does something for you, savor the intention behind it. It will generate the feeling of gratitude in you. I faced a similar situation a few days back. I had to go for an important meeting in the morning and so I requested my maid to come early so that she could do some cooking. She promised to do so, but did not turn up until it was time for me to leave. I became anxious, as I had not cooked for the rest of the family as I was depending on her. I was in a fix and I was getting late. However, I made some arrangements to order food and I as was about to leave, my maid entered. Since I was already agitated, I took her to task, without even listening to her and left home in a frenzy. When I came back I learnt that someone had passed away in her family that morning. She came to work against the wishes of her family members, just because she had promised me. When I heard this, I felt guilty for having reacted that way and my heart was filled with gratitude for her. From that incident onwards, I think twice before reacting.

- **Get in to the habit of appreciation**: This will not only make you grateful, but also transform you into a positive and lovable person. My friend's dad who is 84-year-old, has undergone one by-pass, one cancer surgery and one stroke. But he looks much healthier and happier than so many people of his age. Whenever he speaks he is always appreciating the person he is talking to, or expressing gratitude. He has friends in the age group of twenty to ninety. People love and adore him and long to be in his company. Such is the power of expressing appreciation and gratitude.

Gratitude is like a magic pill. It has the potential of making you healthy, wealthy, happy and successful. So wake up every day and,

- Express gratitude for yet another beautiful day.
- Express gratitude to the people who mean a lot to you, for being there in your life.
- Acknowledge yourself for what you have done and accomplished in the last day/week/month/year. Instead of comparing yourself to others, give yourself credit for the big and small things you have been doing!
- Feel a sense of abundance in your life

- Appreciate and acknowledge the contribution of others to your well-being
- Recognize life's smallest pleasures
- Acknowledge importance of experiencing and expressing gratitude

Make gratitude a way of life. It easily fits into your morning routine; however busy it may be. It will certainly make every day a memorable one and life worthwhile for you and those around you.

This is one of the best ways to make a start to your day. An attitude of gratitude means making it a habit to express thankfulness and appreciation in all parts of your life, on a regular basis, for both the big and small things alike. If you focus on what you have, you will always have more and if you focus on what you don't have, you will never have enough. Everyday may not be perfect but if you develop an attitude of gratitude, it will definitely change your perspective and mindset from negative to positive.

> When you wake up, thank the universe that you are alive.

10

WAKING UP TO LIVE FULLY AND PASSIONATELY

10

Make The Impossible Happen

"You have never lived this day before, you will never live it again, so make the most of it."

- Anonymous -

Do you ever have a feeling that you're drifting through life, and not going where you want to go? Or that you don't know how you got where you are today?

We often find ourselves running from sun-up to sun-down, trying to make the sense of it all and still feel disoriented at the end of the day. In our race against time and trying hard to fulfil our professional and personal commitments, leaves us with a feeling, 'life is out of control'. Although we may exercise, meditate, eat healthy food, motivate ourselves to achieve our goals, somewhere we may experience a void, a sense of unhappiness and discontent in our life if we are not living consciously and passionately.

Living consciously is about taking control of your life and coming out of the auto-pilot mode. It is about having a life that we want rather than settling for the one that befalls us. As we go through the day we may come across several stress inducing situations on the professional and personal front. This stress produces plenty of health issues on a physical, emotional and mental level. The importance of staying fit emotionally, feeling happy, content, passionate about life cannot be ignored. In your morning routine of Fitness, Nutrition, Yoga, Meditation and Motivation, which are the core ingredients, a few add-ons will give a sense of fulfilment

to your being and better control on your life.

1. LAUGH AWAY YOUR WORRIES

Have you seen little children just laughing and giggling at the silliest things? They are in a natural and unconditional state of happiness and bliss.

I have a friend who is a respectable lawyer with a huge practice. His son lives in the United States. He visits them once in two years. He has a five-year-old grand-son; he loves beyond measure. My friend becomes a child in his company, and they together act silly and laugh loudly without any reason; dropping all the inhibitions. Though this friend has a few health issues, they make a temporary exit when he is in the company of his grand-son.

> Living consciously is about taking control of your life and coming out of the auto-pilot mode.

Isn't it amazing how life seems to be so great and perfect, when we enjoy a hearty laugh? Do you remember the last time you have laughed uncontrollably holding your stomach tight? It's been ages, right? As we grow up we distance ourselves from these tiny joys of life. We often wear a façade and hide ourselves behind that. We are governed by the code of conduct of the society and laughing loudly certainly does not fit into it.

Why do they say 'laughter is the best medicine'?

Research says that laughter decreases stress hormones and increases immune cells and infection-fighting antibodies, thus improving your resistance to disease. Laughter triggers the release of endorphins, the body's natural feel-good chemicals. Endorphins promote an overall sense of well-being and can even temporarily relieve pain. Laughter has demonstrated a wealth of physiological, psychological, social, spiritual, and quality-of-life benefits. Increasing numbers of health care centers are adopting laughter therapy as a form of complementary care.

The pressures and demands of work and home can weigh you down with seriousness, and leave you feeling worn-out and hopeless. Laughter makes you feel good. And the good feeling that you get when you laugh remains with you even after the laughter subsides. It gives you a positive, optimistic outlook through difficult situations, disappointments, and loss.

> Laughter has demonstrated a wealth of physiological, psychological, social, spiritual, and quality-of-life benefits.

More than just a respite from sadness and pain, laughter gives you the courage and strength to find new sources of meaning and hope. Even in the most difficult of times, a laugh, or even simply a smile, can go a long way toward making you feel better. And laughter really is contagious, just hearing someone laugh, activates your brain, and readies you to smile and join in the fun.

Laughter is a universal language and can establish a connection between any two strangers encompassing cast, creed, age, sex, nationality. A hearty laugh has the power to dissolve the tension and negative emotions, relax your body, mind and spirit and changes your perspective towards the situation and towards life. It is the most powerful antidote to stress.

In spite of the innumerable benefits, this universal medicine comes absolutely free of cost, it is fun and easy to use. Unfortunately, we fail to call on laughter in the times of need.

Incorporating this wonder drug in to your morning routine can take care of lot of things during the day. Lot of laughter clubs have sprung up which promote this absolutely wonderful medicine. It is also the best exercise for your facial muscles. Humour takes you to a higher place where you can view the world from a more relaxed, positive, creative, joyful, and balanced perspective.

How about adding a dash of humour to your morning routine?

2. AFFIRMATIONS TO KICK-START YOUR DAY

An affirmation is short and positive statement, repeated several times to get the desired results. You must have noticed that some people often keep whining and complaining about their health, relations, finances and about their life in general. Such people always live with something or the other lacking in their life. For instance, if someone says, 'I don't have money', that person can never be rich. The concept is like this. Whatever we repeat gets etched on our sub-conscious mind. Our subconscious mind accepts that as true. Accordingly, it attracts corresponding events, situations or people in our life.

> Whatever we repeat gets etched on our sub-conscious mind. Our subconscious mind accepts that as true. Accordingly, it attracts corresponding events, situations or people in our life.

So why not choose to say, think and live with only positive thoughts, in order to get positive results? For example, if you are looking for good relationships in life and you don't have them at present, your affirmation should be, "I share beautiful and fulfilling relationships with people around me." Starting your day with a positive affirmation and repeating this mentally several times in a day, will manifest that in your life. This can be repeated even when you are doing your routine morning chores and even during your exercise and meditation.

> Massage can be a powerful tool to help you take charge of your health and well-being, whether you have a specific health condition or are just looking for another stress reliever.

If you make positive affirmations a part of your morning routine kit, you are adding a powerful tool that will help you achieve success and the life of your dreams.

Here's a list of 20 affirmations that will help you start your morning on a very positive note. You may choose to repeat one affirmation for any number of times, regularly for 21 days and then move to the next; or you may repeat the whole list of affirmations everyday.

1. I am in full control of my day.
2. Today is the happiest day of my life.
3. Every sunrise brings me good luck.
4. I wake up with a deep sense of love and peace.
5. I share beautiful and fulfilling relationships with people around me.
6. I attract prosperity in my life.

7. I am confident.
8. I am blessed.
9. I am at the pink of my health.
10. I know, I can.
11. I am capable.
12. I am strong.
13. I believe I can.
14. I am courageous.
15. I can easily turn my dreams into reality.
16. I trust my decisions.
17. I am divinely guided through the day.
18. I wake up energised and excited.
19. I attract love in my life.
20. I handle any challenge that arises today with ease.

Repeating these affirmations, every morning, will fill you with peace, calm and positivity and mark a wonderful start for the day.

3. RELAX AND REJUVENATE WITH A MASSAGE

Massage is no longer a domain of a privileged few. Massage is no more available only through luxury spas and upscale health clubs. Today, massage therapy is offered in businesses, clinics, hospitals and even airports.

Getting a massage, can do a world of good for you. If this can be included in your health regime intermittently, it can create wonders for your body. Your morning routine can be slightly altered for Sunday making room for a wholesome massage.

Massage is generally considered part of complementary and alternative medicine. It is increasingly being offered along with standard treatment for a wide range of medical conditions and situations.

Studies of the benefits of massage demonstrate that it is an effective treatment for reducing stress, pain and muscle tension. A body massage primarily has following advantages:

- Reducing or eliminating pain
- Improving joint mobility
- Improving blood circulation
- Improving lymphatic drainage
- Reducing muscular tension
- Greater energy
- Better sleep
- Relaxation of all body parts

If you have any thoughts that massage is only a feel-good way to indulge or pamper yourself, brush it aside. On the contrary, massage can be a powerful tool to help you take charge of your health and well-being, whether you have a specific health condition or are just looking for another stress reliever.

4. ART ENABLES YOU TO FIND YOURSELVES

Simply put, art is a creative expression.

Most of the times as we grow up we stop expressing ourselves. Our lives become so mechanical that we never touch that creative side of us. Creativity can be a way of life. It can be expressed in dressing up, cooking, decorating your house, painting, photography, writing, singing, dancing or anything that you do. Anything that is creatively done does not make it redundant.

When you are creatively involved in something you are operating out of the deeper layers of your mind. Practicing art helps you to be touch with your inner core and to discover yourself.

Make time in your morning routine to be able to appreciate and practice art. If you go for a morning walk, try to go in the nature, observe the surroundings as you walk, appreciate the flora and the fauna, the sky and the nature around. The idea is to develop appreciation for the beauty. If possible, make habit of writing a journal. This will help greatly in expressing yourself. Practice some form of art and if it is not possible on a daily basis, you may incorporate it in the more flexi routine on the weekends. Doing this will help you a great deal in staying emotionally fit, and finding yourself.

> When you are creatively involved in something you are operating out of the deeper layers of your mind. Practicing art helps you to be touch with your inner core and to discover yourself.

It just takes a minute to shift to living life with greater awareness. Make that shift today and wake up to live a passionate and purposeful life. Add these bits to the core ingredients of your morning routine, to energize it.

RISE AND SHINE

11

Head-start Your Day

"No matter how you feel, get up, dress up, show up and never give up!"

Start the night before:

The start of the morning depends on how well you slept the previous night. Also, the night's sleep depends on how you spent your day, which in turn depends on how you started the morning. It is an ongoing cycle. Every person's sleep and wake up cycle is different. If you are a late sleeper, try to go to bed one hour earlier than your usual time, so that you get one hour extra in the morning. An uninterrupted sleep of six to eight hours can act as a foundation for the start of a great morning.

Few tips to ensure that you get a good quality sleep:
- Hit the bed when you are tired
- Switch off all the electronic gadgets including TV and mobile phone
- Put on some soothing music
- Have dim lighting or you can make use of aroma oils in a diffuser
- Do whatever it takes to relax, so that you are fresh to kick-start the morning.

Wake up feeling excited:

Every morning when you wake up ask yourself, "How best I can make use of the day, so that I don't regret that another precious day of my life has passed by." Look forward to a new day as if it is the only day you have. Every day brings with it a new opportunity and helps you take a step towards your goal. Some days you may wake up with lot of excitement while others may be dull. If you wake up with a sulky mood, make an effort to change it. Remember it is only a state of mind that can be easily altered. Use the tips given in this book. Read a motivational quote or do something creative or laugh it out, or say an affirmation or practice gratitude. Doing this can instantly change your mood and prevent it from transforming it into a bad day. It's your day and remember you always have a choice. Exercise your choice and make the most of it. Have a morning routine that sets a positive tone to your day.

Prepare a morning recipe:

Using all the ingredients given in this book, make your own morning recipe. The core, essential ingredients are nutrition, fitness, meditation and motivation. You can garnish it with other elements like laughter, gratitude, affirmations, creativity, massage, music, and art. This will build a power-packed morning recipe.

when you are really tight on time, here is a **24-minute Power-start package** for you, before you do anything else. There are four steps between the time you wake up and face the world.

Step 1: Drink a glass on warm water with lime and honey (2 minutes)

Step 2: Physical Exercise with music – Warm up yoga Stretches (10 minutes)

Step 3: Meditation followed by visualization (8 minutes)

Step 4: Make a smoothie and have it (4 minutes)

We need to remember that life is about striking a balance. Time may not permit us every morning, to do all that is ideal. We are all unique individuals having different life styles, different professions, different body clocks and different purpose. Moreover, we are the best judge of ourselves. Therefore, we need to formulate a recipe best suited to our taste. If we are not too harsh on ourselves, but are disciplined and consistent in what we do, we can certainly take our life to a next level.

So, Wake up with Confidence,

Remember to 'Rise and Shine',

And Have a Great Morning…!

www.ingramcontent.com/pod-product-compliance
Lightning Source LLC
Chambersburg PA
CBHW032126090426
42743CB00007B/490